Playday
To
Payday

Networking and Schmoozing While Caribbean Cruising!

By
Some of the Worlds
Top Marketers

Payday To Playday

Dedication

This book is dedicated to all the Marketers
that have paved the way before us,
are the inspirations for today,
and the ones yet to come.

Payday To Playday

Table of Contents

Forward

Here we are again, sailing on the high-seas with old friends and looking forward to meeting new ones. The countdown starts every year from the moment we set foot on dry land again. 365 days of businesses made easier, all because of the connections made on the Marketers Cruise.

I've said it before, and I'll say it again….Cruising with 400 like-minded people that are in the same boat as you ☺, people that actually understand your business, people that you can actually talk to about your business, and having the opportunity to possibly Joint Venture with 20 or 30 or 100 other entrepreneurs, is something that doesn't happen every day.

The entrepreneurs that join this cruise every January are people that have been successful for many years, to those that have been in business a few short years, to those that are just venturing out. And it's an international cornucopia of the brightest minds in the Internet Marketing world.

Whether you're having a breakfast get-together, sipping a cold one at the bar, dining at a table for 10, or just checking out "Pizza and Profits" at midnight on the Lido Deck, you never know who you will strike up a conversation with. Secrets are let out of the bag, and some of the best relationships, business ventures, and friendships have been forged.

Once again we are privileged to have some of the best of the best share some of their greatest trade secrets for better business. Many of these authors charge thousands of dollars for this information through one-on-one coaching and consulting, but they have been kind enough to leave their egos at the door and share their insights and expertise with their marketing peers.

This is a powerhouse of some of the best in the business, so kick back, read their "words of wisdom," and when you see them walking on the ship, having a drink at the bar, or lounging by the pool, tell them how much you enjoyed their story, and ask them what *you can do for them.*

See you in the JV Jacuzzi or on the Lido Deck for Pizza and Profits!

Carolyn Lewis
"The Book Diva"

Chapter 1

Becoming THE #1 Authority In Your Market

By Mike Lewis

You've been hearing a lot lately about reputation management, image, authority, trust and platform. We are now living in the Age of Reputation, and because of all that, all of these refer in one way or another to "What Does My Customer Think of Me?"

If you're struggling to build a targeted list, command higher prices, get more referrals, attract JV partners or earn leveraged income, than I'm willing to bet that the lack of being the clear expert in your niche is your biggest problem.

Before you can say for sure who you want to be, answer these 7 Questions:

1. Who are you?
2. Why should I trust you?
3. What are you selling?
4. What's in it for me?
5. When can I expect results?
6. How much is it going to cost?
7. What do I need to do next?

Remember that it all starts with, and goes back to, doing business with the best experts, the people that you know, like and trust.

How Would Your Life Change If You Became THE #1 Authority In Your Market?

What I have to share is a practical system that helps people like you – people who have a massive message for the world – to become THE #1 Authority in Your Market.

Payday To Playday

I believe that the following are necessary to increase your success. Remember, the more that you have completed, the more trust and authority it's going to give you in the buyer's eyes:

1. **Cleaning up social media**

   Do you think that only your friends and family are seeing your postings? Well, guess again. 45% of employers are currently using social media sites prior to hiring candidates. They are now going on LinkedIn, Twitter and Facebook to find out if said candidate would be a good fit for their company. If employers are forward enough to check you out, don't you think that prospective customers and JV partners are also doing the same?

   Let's take a look at some of the reasons why you might be rejected:
   1) Poor communication skills
   2) Confidential information is being shared
   3) Inappropriate information or pictures are posted
   4) Bad-mouthing clients or co-workers
   5) Qualifications are incorrect

   Now on the flip side, here are some reasons why you might be accepted:
   1) Great communication skills
   2) Supported qualifications
   3) Positive references or comments posted about you
   4) Your creativity shows through
   5) Well-rounded

   Keep in mind that it is your responsibility to show the best of you. No matter what others write about you, it doesn't even come close to who you actually are, because no one knows you better than yourself.

2. **Your Trademark Speech**

   If I told you that you had just 3 seconds to convince a prospect to listen to what you had to say, would that change the way you thought about your brand? I hope so.

   Everything you do must convey your entire message, brand and authenticity within those precious 3 seconds, quickly and effortlessly in your prospect's head.

   Not only can we show you the best ways to do this, we will also help get your prospects excited to learn more about how you can help THEM.

3. **Coaching Programs**

   Running a business can be overwhelming. Many owners are finding it difficult to keep up with the ever-changing market, satisfying their current customers, and prospecting for new ones.

   Many find that having a business coach is critical. It's like having a baseball or tennis coach: they are there to provide support, develop strategies, help maximize your performance, listen to you, tell you the truth and basically keep you in line and in the game.

   Business owners who are out-going, results-oriented, self-aware, and willing and able to develop a strategic plan to grow their business into a profitable business engine that will run without them are the type of clients that coaches want to work with.

   The purpose of a coach is to help you focus and bring your

business to the next level. They can help you with:

1) Business Development
2) Marketing Strategies
3) Leadership Training
4) Strategic Plan
5) Finances
6) Systems
7) Advertising
8) Team Development
9) Sales Management
10) Tactics and Strategies

4. Live Events

It's great to be able to work from the comfort of our own home, but we tend to get into a rut, stay indoors working for hours on end, until the walls start closing in on us. Now I know that you generally love your own company, and definitely your family, but sometimes we need more!

You need to get out and socialize with like-minded people. And what better place to do it than at a live event?

Attending live events as often as possible is so important. Let's look at some of the significant reasons why:

1. It get you out of your comfort zone
2. You meet potential clients, team members or customers
3. You get a different perspective
4. It lets you spend time with like-minded people

5. You are able to talk with vendors that otherwise you may not even know about
6. You meet amazing people that you normally wouldn't meet in an office or online
7. It helps you to get motivated
8. It deepens existing relationships
9. You are better likely to "Sell" yourself in person
10. It lets you catch up with old friends

5. Membership Sites

If you're an expert in your niche, creating a membership site can leverage your time significantly. But what exactly is a membership site? It's basically a site with specific areas for members. They can be fee free, or members will pay a monthly or annually fee. The main advantage to having a membership site for the affiliate is, of course, the recurring income.

One of the most important keys to the success of your membership site is your sales page. It is generally the first thing your potential members will read prior to joining. So taking the time to create the perfect sales page for your membership site could mean the difference between making enough to only pay your electric bill, to raising your business to 6 figures or more.

6. Publishing

Become the "heavy hitter" that everyone will remember.

If you want to build your reputation and authority, increase your credibility, define your identity, and amplify your name recognition, (even though I listed this one last) then becoming a published author is one of the first steps to being the number one authority in your market.

I'm not just talking about having your own book, I'm also talking about:
1) Sponsored Multi Author Books
2) Multi-author host books
3) Single author 'done for you' books
4) Event books
5) E-books
6) Work books – E-books and physical
7) Audio programs - E-books and physical
8) Video programs - E-books and physical
9) Complete 'done for you' information products
10) 'Done for you' webinars, both live and automated

So what will being a part of the publishing business do for you? It will:
1) Definitely build your reputation and authority, increase your credibility, define your identity, and amplify your name recognition
2) Cultivate marketing, speaking engagements, public relations, joint venture partners, etc.
3) Help create a profitable business-building program
4) Build Platforms and Create additional profit streams
5) Get your message out, develop a fan base, and assist in your business' growth
6) Create multi-media products and materials

I invite you to take advantage of our expert experience. We offer full-scale white label publishing services, from editorial development to production, as well as additional marketing opportunities that will suit your needs and support your ultimate goal of become an acclaimed authority.

Payday To Playday

About Mike Lewis, *"The Book Guy"*

Mike has over 35 years of experience in marketing, finance, construction and real estate. He previously owned and operated several companies in the southeast, including a $100 million land development company.

He is the owner / publisher of Nomad CEO, the top Ghost Publishing firm in the world, specializing in books, tools, and resources for entrepreneurship and small businesses.

His products are practical, hands-on, and based on the real-world experiences of successful entrepreneurs, CEOs, investors, lenders, and seasoned business experts.

Mike's passion for turning non-writers into authors of printed books in less than 30 days, with virtually no writing on their part, positively impacts and changes lives.

Using his complete "Done For You" publishing service has helped raise his client-author's authority and recognition in all phases of their businesses.

Check out Mike's website at **www.nomadceo.com,** or contact him directly at mlewis@nomadceo.com for information on how you, too, can become the expert in your field through the power of becoming a published author.

"The aim of marketing is to know and understand the customer so well the product or service fits him and sells itself."

~Peter Drucker~

Chapter 2

CRUISING FOR PROFITS?
Just Add Water!

By Capt. Lou

Woody Allen said 80% of success is just showing up. It was way back in January of 2003 that I took his advice and attended my very first internet marketing conference called "The BIG Seminar" in Dallas, Texas.

I had hoped to learn how to put my local "Little Shop of Cruises" travel agency online and reach out to a greater audience via the web.

Never did I imagine that the people I would meet there that weekend would profoundly change my business model, and the course of my LIFE!

It was another marketer in attendance that asked if I could arrange a similar event on a cruise ship, sort of a "seminar-at-sea" combined with a fun vacation vibe.

She asked if we could do mastermind meetings and JVs in a giant Jacuzzi, sipping a Pina colada, while sailing away from some sun-drenched island in the Bahamas or Caribbean?

Not even realizing that JV stood for "joint venture", I instantly said SURE, if you want to "cruise for profits"...JUST ADD WATER!

At that event, I bought all the info products and software packages and discovered how to automate the booking process online, and how to finally stop selling one-on-one by phone, and start selling one-on-many through websites, webinars, live stage presentations, etc.

On Halloween weekend of 2003, my first "special-event-at-sea" debuted with about 50 students and speakers. We did just about everything wrong and yet it was a HUGE success.

It was that "Affiliate Marketers Cruise" that led to me transforming my business model away from one of a million travel agencies, to being a one IN a million producer / planner of specialty themed niche group vacations.

Branding myself as "Captain Lou" the cruise-guru worked very well, and I quickly became THE go-to guy for niche marketers with audiences they wanted to WOW with an unforgettable, profitable and life-changing experience.

I started producing "Special-Events-At-Sea" for casino chip collectors, murder mystery writers, opera groups, multi-generational family reunions, real estate trainers, marketing coaches, consultants and gurus.

In January of 2007, I showed up again, at Mike Filsaime's $5,000 live event called the 7-figure Code. Mike has been a guest on some of our previous cruises and was starting to become more of a friend than a client.

His idea was to continue these cruises, but in a bigger way, with a much bigger vision.

The Marketers Cruise would be a no speakers, no selling, NOT a seminar-at-sea that is guru-student, but rather a true peer-to-peer networking and mastermind vacation that would draw the world's TOP marketers for an adventure of a lifetime that happens every January.

Instead of adding a $1,000 to $5,000 event fee for attendees, which I do with many of my niche cruise events, our give back to the internet marketing community that has done so much for our businesses, would be to keep the Marketers Cruise at our costs!

Making it affordable, profitable and FUN for everyone to attend and bring their family and friends. The rest is history. Over the past several years, we've gone from 61 to 118 to 263 to over 400 attendees each January. Top VIP marketers who've put everything on hold to come join our cruise family include:

Mike Filsaime & Donna Fox (your hosts)
Robert Allen
Rich Schefren
Matt Bacak
James Malenchak
Russell Brunson
Ted Thomas
Joel Peterson
David Cavanagh
Jeff Mills
Daven Michaels
Joel Therien
Armando Montelongo
and many other top names, including the publishers of this book, Mike & Carolyn Lewis, and the many entrepreneurial CEO's who have contributed chapters about their personal marketing voyage.

The Marketers Cruise is my "flagship" product. It is what's turned "Captain WHO?" into "Captain Lou."

This event, where profitable deals are done while on vacation and having fun, has been the springboard for my Million-Dollar Groups System info-product, a $2,000 training course for cruise agents that has been flying off the shelves.

When I'm not speaking at travel industry events, I help develop groups for niche marketers who either want to bring their own audience on the Marketers Cruise or ANY cruise ship adventure to the Caribbean, Alaska, Hawaii, or Europe...instead of some stuffy hotel conference room.

Remember that to BE un-shoppable you need to be one in a million, not one *OF* a million. Carnival cruise lines have done a great job selling FUN. Make whatever you are selling an EXPERIENCE that's fun, and cool, with your own version of the "Champagne and Strawberries" at embarkation.

Your clients will never want to leave, and they'll keep coming back for more. Then one day, your industries' top leaders may tap YOU on the shoulders and ask if YOU would like to do a profitable joint venture with them, just like Mike Filsaime did with Donna Fox and Captain Lou.

MarketersGoneWild.com

Payday To Playday

About Captain Lou

Captain Lou has 30+ years of sales and marketing experience, offline and online, b to c and b to b. He considers himself "psychologically unemployable". After getting fired 5 times in a row, Captain Lou built several 7-figure sales operations from scratch on little more than an 8th grade education and fire in the belly. His goals are to travel the world, not only fulfilling his own dreams and fantasies, but also those of his clients.

Captain Lou prides himself in showing niche group leaders how to cruise the world for free, with their own highly profitable "Special-Events-At-Sea".

He is the Creator of CruiseMarketingMagic.com and the Million-Dollar-Groups-System for travel sellers, as well as the Producer / Planner of the amazing annual internet marketer's mastermind and networking vacation known as: **http://MarketersCruise.com**

For more information, check out Captain Lou at:
http://CaptainLou.com or http://SpecialEventsAtSea.com

Chapter 3

Creating Your New Wealth
& Freedom Lifestyle

By Daven Michaels

My entrepreneurial career started at the age of 15 with a dream to have a designer clothing retail store on Melrose Street in Los Angeles. Being so young I was turned down by everyone I knew for the start-up capital, so I turned to my supportive father for the money I needed.

My grand opening was a traditional Hollywood style fanfare, champagne flowing, cheers and slaps on the back. The days that followed were the most nervous days of my life! For the next few days I had no customers, not one! I recall feeling extremely anxious and worried; what if I had failed before I even started! I remember thinking about the money I had borrowed and how long it would take me to pay back my Dad. Even in those nervous anxious moments, in my heart I still knew I could make this work. I had to make this work. As fate would have it, by the end of first week Jack Nicholson bought out half my shop and I was in business! From that moment I knew I would always be an entrepreneur and I have never looked back.

I have truly lived the American Dream. I have turned multiple passions into prosperous businesses. I have been a bestselling music and television producer, author, speaker and successful entrepreneur. I have worked hard, played hard, travelled the world, and been involved with incredible people, amazing projects and exciting ventures. Some say I have been lucky, and maybe I have. However, very early on in my entrepreneurial career I became aware of a formula for success that I attribute my ability to turn multiple diverse businesses into financial success.

I first became aware of a success formula during my time as a record producer; I discovered that there is a formula for creating hit records. This made me think there must be a success formula for running a business. I actively sought out mentors who I knew were successful, and through their mentorship I developed a formula for success that I now teach to others!

In addition to running 123Employee, what I really enjoy doing is helping small business owners around the world create their new wealth and freedom lifestyle by showing them how to effectively leverage and delegate. Money alone does not translate into success. I know many rich people who are unhappy; they work long hours and are miserable. The definition of success, wealth and freedom are relative. My definition of success, wealth and freedom may be totally different from yours. My definition is simple; it's having the resources to live the lifestyle you desire, and being happy.

While I achieved financial success in my businesses early on, I did not achieve freedom and expansion until I fully understood and embraced how to effectively 'Delegate' and 'Leverage'. No successful person has been able to establish a business without mastering these two core concepts. Learning how to delegate is the bridge between self-employed and being a business owner, and yet, this is often easier said than done!

I think one of the reasons I am able to relate to "soletrepreneurs" and small business owners is that many of them tend to micromanage, and I was one as well. Even today, my staff has to wrestle tasks off me, so I know how most people feel about hiring people to help them and then assigning tasks consistently to make an impact in the business.

Even though I manage a staff of 400 people, I still work from home. My management team and staff are all virtual, and I still consider myself a small-business owner, working with the same challenges as many entrepreneurs and small businesses who are my clients. Many key aspects of my business are delegated to employees all over the world, and this makes me uniquely positioned to share my experience with others.

Outsourcing is a form of delegation which is commonly understood as hiring people from countries like India, Philippines, and Eastern-Europe to do tasks for you. And while that is the common understanding, I believe we live in a global economy that is not limited by boundaries, nationalities, or cultures. When I use the word 'outsourcing' today, I think of assigning the task to anyone outside your company, regardless of geographical location.

Over time we have created a simple methodology for how to effectively create a delegation plan, which we call:

The 7 Steps to Successful Delegation

Step1: Deciding What To Delegate

The first step in creating a delegation plan is creating a delegation table for **EACH** project/income stream as follows:

1) Take a sheet of paper (landscape). Create 4 columns on a sheet of paper, and label as follows:
   - Column 1 : List the Tasks YOU HAVE TO DO
   - Column 2 : List the Tasks you HAVE TO outsource to others (you don't have the skill)
   - Column 3 : List the Tasks you are doing that could be done by others
   - Column 4 : List the Task you would be doing if you had more time or money
2) Divide the columns into 2 rows and label as 'Marketing Related Tasks' & 'All Other Tasks'
3) Enter all the tasks related to a project/income stream into the table.

Step2: Prioritizing What Tasks To Delegate First

In an ideal world it would be great to outsource EVERYTHING you don't have to do or want to do... the reality is that we are all limited by resources, and we have to prioritize what tasks to outsource first.

1) **MUST OUTSOURCE NEXT**

   These are task or projects you MUST outsource next in order for your business to proceed. It could be the creation of a website, lead capture page, sales page, or copywriting. In most cases the MUST do list are things you are not able to do, or don't have time for and have to hire someone to do them for you. In many cases these tasks may be project based.

2) **MARKETING TO INCREASE REVENUE**

   The next set of tasks I would outsource should lead to the generation of more sales. This would mean either:

- Hiring someone to generate more leads for you
- Delegating the bust task you are doing so that YOU can generate more sales.

We often advise our clients to implement an outsourcing strategy to hire someone to generate more leads via internet marketing, social media or telemarketing. While this might apply for many businesses, there are some instances where our client is a great sales person themselves and simply needs more time to make calls, attend networking events, talk at events, etc. In this scenario, we would look to identify tasks you are doing that can be outsourced so that you have more time to do what you are BEST at!

3) **OUTSOURCE YOUR DISLIKE LIST, NOT GOOD AT & BORING TASK LIST**

Once you have outsourced 'must do & marketing tasks', you can outsource your 'dislike', 'not good at', and 'boring and mundane' tasks you really do not want to do.

Step3: Selecting Who To Delegate To

Often new prospects will want to hire a $6 per hour VA, and what they are really looking for is a consultant, specialist or business/project manager. Knowing who to hire for the right job is crucial for your success. Once you have completed the table, assign the tasks to one of the following:

- **Consultant:** Someone who will advise you, create a strategy or plan of action. They typically do not do the work themselves.

21

- **Specialist:** Someone with specialized skills (graphics, web, technology, consultant, accountant, etc.)
- **Business/Project Manager**: Manages key aspects of your business
- **In-house Employee:** Someone who comes into your place of business, full or part time
- **Remote Employee:** Someone who works remotely

Step4: Instructing How You Want The Task Done

Once you have identified the tasks to delegate, prioritized the tasks, and decided who to assign the tasks to, the next step is to create **B**asic **O**perational **S**equential **S**teps

The instructions should be simple, step-by-step, and easy to follow. If you do not know how to do certain tasks, ask your agent to research or review any applicable training material.

Instructions can be as simple as writing the steps in a word document, audio recording of phone calls, scripts trees, creating training videos and using screen capture software.

Step 5: Allocating When You Want The Task Done

In addition to providing instructions, we recommend you create a schedule and allocate time for different tasks throughout the week in Google Calendar or a similar program. This is often overlooked, often because you are too busy and don't have time to create the calendar for your employees. However, when the time is taken upfront, the results are improved.

Step 6: Understanding Why Outsourcing Might Now Work

Many people complain that outsourcing did not work for them, and they often blame their virtual employee or service provider. The reality is that there are six key aspects to outsourcing, which we refer to as the 6 pillars of successful outsourcing:

1) The business is not well defined or structured. The funnels, websites, copy, are not great...
2) The employers do not know how to communicate or manage, which overwhelms the VA...
3) The tasks are not appropriate for that level employee...
4) The instructions are not clear...
5) The employee/agent is not up to the task...
6) The employer has unrealistic expectations from their agent

When these reasons are adequately addressed, the better the outsourcing relationship will be.

Step 7: Know Your Role

Once you have made the decision to outsource and used the delegation process to decide what to outsource you will first need to get through the first 30-90 days. We do our best to assist our clients with this process. The reality is that they are YOUR employee working in our facility under our care and management. It is important you know your role in the process; they are your employee and will look to you for advice and guidance. Provide information and resources to allow their tasks to be done.

Payday To Playday

About Daven Michaels

Daven Michaels presents innovative marketing strategies to entrepreneurs and business leaders all over the globe year after year. Aside from being a dynamic business and personal development trainer, he is the founder and CEO of 123Employee, the premiere outsourcing center in the Philippines, with hundreds of employees working thousands of hours per day for freedom-starved entrepreneurs worldwide.

Daven is also the brains behind the 'New Wealth & Freedom' system, while also being an in-demand speaker. In addition, he travels the globe educating entrepreneurs about the benefits of outsourcing and the importance of delegation.

Many personal development trainers talk about making more money, working less, turning your passion into prosperity, having more time and freedom, and many sell great info products. Daven does more than talk about it, though: he has lived it, breathes it, teaches his success formula and strategies, and through 123Employee services helps entrepreneurs all over the world make more money, save valuable time and create the lifestyle they dream about.

Daven Michaels has been labeled a 'Super Entrepreneur' by the media and his associates. Daven, who has been an entrepreneur since the age of 15, has enjoyed successful careers in the designer clothes retail industry, music promotion for crowds, and an award winning career as a music and TV producer.

Daven models the lifestyle he inspires, managing hundreds of employees with only a laptop and internet connection.

Now he devotes his energies to helping others discover the freedom of outsourcing as the CEO of 123Employee.

"One of the keys to success is 'Market Like M.A.D.' (Multiple Methods, Automation, Delegation)."
-Daven Michaels

Check out Daven at www.123Employee.com

"Affiliate marketing has made businesses millions and ordinary people millionaires."

~Bo Bennett~

Chapter 4

The Trinity Success Method

by Tom Beal

Do you desire more Joy, Adventure, and Passion in your life? How about peace, love, and happiness, all topped off with an incredible lifestyle filled with extreme gratitude.

Recently, after finding myself procrastinating, and asking myself why I was not taking the actions I knew I should be, it hit me. I was overcomplicating things!

I was not confident of what my next steps to take were, and in that lack of confidence my belief in actually being able to attain the goals I had was slim at best, which would make it virtually impossible to attain.

So I went back to the basics and uncovered this epiphany that simplified not only my immediate goals at hand, but success in life at all levels in a way I had never heard or experienced before.

Almost as if my hand was being controlled by someone or something other than me, I began to draw triangles on a large pad and then attach words to each side of those 7 triangles, and when I was done had a euphoric feeling and felt like yelling "Eureka!"

This was a good one, and if explained properly can greatly assist you right now in taking your life and results to a whole new level.

Strangely, this all happened on the 4th anniversary of the passing of my Dad, at 56, just a few weeks prior to me finally sitting down and writing out this new epiphany for you, right now.

By the way, for immediate validation of what I just described to you, here is the video that I created on that day, plus a picture of those 7 triangles I am about to reveal to you now:

http://tombeal.com/4yearsago

This is my first attempt at putting this into words, and it is my hope I will be able to do it in a way that has a positive and lasting impact on your life.

Here we go...

Grab a pen and a piece of paper and then draw an equilateral triangle in the center of the page.

Below the base of the triangle write Health, to the outside of the left side, write Relationships, and on the outside of the right hand side, write Financial.

True Success is a balance of all three sides of that triangle: Health, Relationships, and Finances.

One without the others hampers true joy, adventure, peace, happiness, fulfillment, purpose, and passion.

Here's the rub: rarely are, or can all three be absolutely perfect.

Life would be boring without chaos. Think about it.

Where and how could we grow and explore without chaos. We can either choose to make a game of it and seek solutions to the chaos that arises, or fret, worry or complain about it. I know you choose the prior, or else you wouldn't have come across this book, or read this far, and I commend you for being an action taker.

Payday To Playday

So, back to the True Success Triangle...

Generally there is one of the sides that demands the lion's share of your attention, and in many cases two of the three may be in a bit of a mess, and occasionally all three can be in shambles.

We all have Winters and Summers. Times of ease & flow, and times of pain & difficulty.

Good and bad are just labels we as humans made up to define moments that in the entire of scope of time, just are. It's the meanings we attach to those moments and how we choose to act in all of them that determine our happiness in the moment that matters the most, the now.

Back to your piece of paper. Time to draw another Triangle. This time draw a small arrow below the Health base that leads to another Triangle. On the second triangle below the first one, write in these three words for the base then left and right: Spiritual/Emotional, Mental, and Physical.

To have true health, we need clarity and control of our mind, a fit and working body, and emotional vitality to include recognition that there's more happening than our 3-dimensional body and 5 senses can ever know...and be alright with that.

Now to the left side of the original triangle, Relationships. Draw a short line that leads to another triangle and label each side as: Personal, Professional, and Social.

Relationships will be our greatest joys or miseries in this journey, and it all depends on how we choose to treat them. The first and most important relationship you can cultivate is the one with you and your 'self.' I challenge and dare you to become a person you are proud of. Become the person who knows that if more people were like you, this world would be a better place. Be a good friend to your 'self,' then be a good friend to others.

I know many people, including top performers, who beat themselves up relentlessly, and would never speak to anyone the way they speak to themselves. Sure, we must learn to push ourselves, but we must also learn to do it lovingly and tactfully...as we would to our best friend. Become your best friend. And watch how many others will also want to have you as their best friend, too.

Professional and social relationships are also a huge determining factor to your overall happiness and success. We live in a day and age where meeting one person who sees the value you can contribute to them can change every aspect of your life.

Your family and love life plays a huge part in life enjoyment or misery. And there will be times of joy and pain in these areas. One thing you want to keep top of mind in dealing with your family and loved ones is that this journey is brief, regardless of how long we remain breathing!

None of us have a guarantee of another day, week, month, or year. Be sure to get over grudges with family members and key relationships sooner than later. Those are ridiculous to hold on to, and are like drinking poison, hoping the other person dies. It is just not worth it. Call them, write them, forgive them, and move on. Sometimes you may not continue to spend time with them, but don't spend time in your mind focusing on negative memories, or current outrageous happenings either.

Ok, on to the third side of the original triangle, Finances. Draw a brief arrow from that side to a new triangle you draw with these 3 words around them starting from the base, then left to right: Today, Tomorrow, and Contribution.

In business I break down all of my projects to fit into either Today or Tomorrow money categories. Today means it can and will generate revenue, income, and profits within 30 days...to keep all of my bills and expenses paid which support my lifestyle.

Tomorrow money projects are the larger ones which are capable of bringing in bigger results, but take more time to put them together. These are always helpful to take you to the next level with a large cash inflow for the projects that work.

No risk, no reward. Goal is to make calculated risks with good judgment and discernment. It's all a hypothesis that needs to constantly be tweaked, revised, and updated based upon new information.

Contributions have always amazed me. When you find yourself giving back whatever you're capable of (time or money) to people and charities in need, it opens doors, and sometimes flood gates, that you would have never expected or dreamed of.

Be sure that when you contribute, give with zero ulterior motives in mind. Give because of the good feelings it gives you, to include gratitude for being able to give, and the help it brings to others, no matter how much or how little that giving is. It's not about the size of the gift, it's about your capability and willingness to give from a pure heart.

So I challenge you to do a current assessment of your True Success level right now at this moment.

On a scale of 1 to 10, with 1 being lowest and 10 being highest, where would you rate your

- Health:
- Relationships:
- Finances:

That is your starting point, and it may be a different rating for you on a daily, weekly, and monthly basis, depending upon the happenings in your life.

The next step is to ask your 'self' for each of those three areas, these questions:

- Where would you like it to be in this area, within the next 12 months?
- How are you going to make that happen?
- What must take place to get you from where you are to where you want to be?
- By when will this occur?
- When are you going to begin?

Congratulations! You are now on a proper, simplified path to getting from where you are to where you want to go.

Now it's time to go back to the initial center True Success Triangle, and this time we are going to write in the only three things that you can control on this journey.

Starting on the inside base of the triangle, to the left, then right, write in: Thoughts, Words, and Actions.

Those are how you are going to transform every aspect of your life, starting now. It begins by recognizing that EVERY thing you choose to Think, Speak, and Do is either bringing you closer to or further from your desired outcomes.

The kicker is that it is the small, seemingly insignificant choices about what you think, say, and do, regularly and consistently that fast track you to your goals or to 180 degrees from your goals, and that choice is all yours.

Here are some questions that will help you stay focused on the proper thoughts, words, and actions:

1) What is my desired outcome? (This is now your daily power question.)

   Ask this at the beginning of each day, and prior to personal & professional "events" that are important, such as: phone calls, meetings, trips, presentations, etc.

   First thing in the morning, you will want to consciously set a desired outcome to do something that progresses your life and success in the 3 areas we discussed today: health, relationships, and finances.
   What am I going to do today that will improve my health? I will choose to eat healthy & nutritious foods, move a lot by (whatever you choose to do that day: walking, running, biking, swimming, stair master, yoga, Pilates, etc.), stay well hydrated and get proper sleep.

   What am I going to do to improve my relationships today? How can I make the lives of the people I care about and come in contact with feel special today? Who do I need to call, text, email, Face Time, or Skype today? How can I make their day better?

What am I going to do to improve my finances today? I will choose to be observant to what I spend my money on today, minimizing impulse purchases, asking myself if I really need this, or am just considering buying it out of boredom? Where is my next sale coming from? Where can I get more potential prospects from? What value can I provide my customers and following? What solution can I provide?

This daily power question is especially helpful to ask yourself when you feel your emotions rising.

When a potential argument begins, and you feel your emotions rising, you will want to recognize that this situation is important to you, since you feel your emotions rising. Then you calmly ask yourself in your mind, "What is my desired outcome in this situation?"

This combined with not taking the situation personally or making assumptions about the other person or this situation as a whole can help you remain calm to not think, say, or do things that you'll later regret.

You may even catch yourself, then state to the other person or people calmly, "My desired outcome for this situation is to..." then state a common ground that all parties would agree to as a desired outcome, "...do you agree that is a good goal for us to go for today?" then get back to making that happen, versus fighting or arguing, which would pull you far from your ideal desired outcome.

2) Is this the best use of my time right now?

If yes, keep doing it; if no, what are 3 options of what you could do right now? Which is my absolute best option?

Just as we have focused on triangles in this exercise, narrowing your possibilities down to the top 3 highly cuts back on overwhelm and procrastination.

So let's recap our Trinity Success Method that we reviewed today:

- Success = health, relationships, finances
- Health = spiritual/emotional, mental, physical
- Relationships = personal, professional, social

All while searching for: Joy, Adventure, Passion, and: Love, Peace & Happiness on this brief and exciting journey.

Only three things we can control in this life is our: thoughts, words, & actions.

About Tom Beal

Tom Beal, known as The Guru Behind the Guru's, is the creator of The Success Magnet System & The Trilogy Success Method. As Founder of Remarkable Marketing, Inc., he speaks all over the world, sometimes in a Mankini, and assists people in getting their marketing remarkable while bringing their lives and results to new levels. Connect at: www.TomBeal.com or email to tom@tombeal.com

If you would also like to get information on Tom's final triangle, visit

http://tombeal.com/4yearsago

Chapter 5

How You Can Double Your Consulting Revenue, Grow Your Net Worth and Have Fun Doing It!

By Jason Myers

If you consult with business owners, read on.

If you know business owners, read on.

If you own a business, read on.

It all started with an idea and a desire to help people. I was speaking at a conference and met a gentleman that had experience in the Private Equity arena. We began to compare notes.

We found that we had similar and compatible desires to help grow businesses, create jobs and grow net worth for everyone involved. The solution seemed simple to us – marry the best of Private Equity and investing with top shelf talent and together this human and financial capital combination could drive measurable success for those involved.

See, the issue with investing in businesses is that the management believes that money will solve their issues. Money helps, but money can also hurt. In fact, money given to the wrong organization or at the wrong time or with the wrong expectations can actually hurt their growth.

Perhaps you've seen it in person or on television. A founder goes out to the investment world (Family, Friends, Angel Investors, Venture Capital, Private Equity or Lenders) and secures capital.

37

Now the real issues begin. The business sets out to spend the money raised by hiring people, buying systems and general and administrative expenses. They raised the capital based on a plan to grow. However, the risk comes in as soon as they invest in something they do not know anything about. Let me give you some examples.

They go out to hire a marketing person, because they need marketing and admittedly know nothing about it. If they know nothing about successful marketing, how can they recruit and hire the best?

They invest in a Customer Relationship Management (CRM) system. Yet, they have never selected one before and they spend 3 months trying to learn the new system only to find that it does not meet their real needs.

They asked for money to build a mobile application and feel it is critical for their growth. They bid out the development and select the lowest qualified bidder. That's what they heard they should do. It was likely that any of the three could have completed the project successfully. However, the project goes bad. The application is a failure and they blame the developer. The real issue was that they needed a software project manager.

The common theme here is that the business owner and their management team are naïve, ignorant and just plain unaware of what they don't know.

When we created CXO Collective, the goal was to mitigate risk by assembling the best of talent and pairing that to investments in companies. In others words, greatly reduce the execution risk caused by poor hiring and selection processes and poor project management.

Are you starting to see the magic here? We have a formula for success that can be leveraged in virtually any organization, regardless of sector or size.

How does this relate to your income, wealth and business? Read on...

We created a framework to allow those who join us to tap into a global network of professionals, advisors, consultants and investors.

If you need help, they are a call or email away.

We created a membership structure where we operate local chapters across the US, and we are expanding globally. Our members have access to the entire network. Our members are investors, consultants, professionals and more.

When we acquire a company, we leverage a process called a BTS. It is a Breakthrough Session. In this BTS we will create a strategic direction and the tactical action items to move the company swiftly to the next level.

As a member, you can participate as a consultant and get paid for participation. We assemble the team based upon the company's declared issues. From there we work to create an actionable plan that will truly drive the business along a path of a highly focused execution.

Do you want to double your consulting revenue? Here goes:

Tap into our network of members and then leverage them to help your existing clients. As an example, let's say you offer Social

Media Consulting/Services. As you are working with a client, it becomes readily obvious to you that they need all of the following: CFO, Search Engine Marketing, Marketing Automation and some help raising capital.

This is where our model pours cash into your pockets. You take advantage of the one-stop shop of CXO by bringing the client's situation to CXO Collective. We provide a short list of resources on the Five areas of specialization. They engage our members and you get an override or revenue share on their engagements.

So, instead of making $5k a month on Social Media from them, you make that $5k, plus $1k per resource. This is another $5k a month. The great thing is $5k a month more, for no more work, is like free money. The client loves you because now you are a trusted advisor helping them solve their toughest business challenges. You have a client for the long haul!

How would you like to grow you net worth – said another way – your Wealth?!

Our model gets even more magical...

The part-time CFO position they hired is compensated with consulting fees (in which you share), performance based incentives (which you get a share of) and Equity Stock Options, which you also share in. So, as the company succeeds, your Stock is worth more and more until at some point the business has a liquidity event (sale or investment) and you get a big payday! The beauty of this is that you are growing your wealth – passively. It is totally incremental to your daily business focus of Social Media consulting.

To recap, you can easily double your consulting revenue by being the one who leverages the Collective to solve your clients' issues. Rather than tell them they need this resource and to go find some. You are the solution... a true one-stop shop. You become a HUGE consulting practice by extension with no overhead or recruiting. Then on top of that, you can earn equity in businesses. Imagine getting a percentage of every business that you provide consulting to. This is without renegotiating your agreement with the client. It all happens on the supplemental resources side (CFO, etc.)

This can be life changing.

All you have to do is to join CXO Collective and engage. The organization will provide access to opportunities. You will provide opportunities for other members, and the circle is completed. Everyone gets the chance to play at a higher level while earning more and building wealth along the way.

On top of all of that, and as a Bonus, if you source a company we can acquire you can earn equity in that deal as a principal (owner). We give you the opportunity to become an owner in the business for helping us to get the "Deal" done.

Some members simply focus on sourcing deals, others focus on BTS sessions, and others focus on tapping our network to bolster their income from partnering/referring business into the Collective, while others just invest in deals.

We have created a movement, a movement towards a smarter way to buy, build and sell companies. If you are like most, this resonates with you. It is time to join us.

Payday To Playday

About Jason Myers

Jason is a pilot, inventor, serial entrepreneur, author, and perpetual sponge for knowledge. He has founded countless successful offline and online companies since 1991.

Most recently, Jason has Co-founded CXO Collective, a Private Equity firm dedicated to world-class execution. CXO Collective is a National Membership organization that harnesses the triad of Capital, Talent and Opportunities. CXO focuses on Buying, Building and Selling its companies.

CXO Collective has grown local chapters in 13 U.S. cities and is expanding internationally. Members earn consulting fees, performance based incentives and stock where the company's CXO is involved in.

To JOIN, go to **http://www.cxocollective.com/join**

For questions, contact Jason at **jason.myers@cxocollective.com**

Chapter 6

Hype And Reality
The Good.. The Bad.. and The Ugly..
By Raam Anand

The Merriam-Webster dictionary defines "hype" as:

(Noun) Extravagant or intensive publicity or promotion.
(Verb) Promote or publicize (a product or idea) intensively,
often exaggerating its importance or benefits; Stimulate or
excite (someone): "I was hyped up because I wanted to do
well."

If you have been on the Internet for some time, I'm sure you have seen a lot of 'hype' going around. This is especially easy to spot in the information and marketing industry.

Tricky marketers use several mechanisms and methods to create 'hype'. In fact, there are even courses and seminars that teach people how to create 'hype' disguised as marketing strategies. Some of these courses became highly popular and helped their creators' make millions of dollars in sales within a few days of their launch. Hype helped make money! But, not all those who purchased the product were able to replicate the same success. That's a different story.

Let's begin by identifying some of the most popular hypes that are making the rounds:

SCARCITY

In a recent article in TIME Magazine titled "How Scarcity Leads to Spending" Maia Szalavitz explains how economic uncertainty and exposure to scarcity makes people want to spend more and risk more. This article was based on a research report published in

Psychological Science magazine to help explain why poverty can sometimes be so difficult to escape.

Scarcity is a psychological trigger that unethical marketers use to influence their prospects to buy from them. This is very much prevalent in the online marketing industry, and it is one of the reasons for many successful product-launches online.

The basic definition of scarcity is "having fewer resources than needed to fill human wants and needs."

There are indeed certain resources that are scarce. In this context, for example, time is a limited resource. If someone is trading their time, then they can say it is scarce because there is only a limited availability of 'time'. On the other hand, you see many "online programs," information products, eBooks, home-study courses and even seminars using the scarcity trick.

EBooks can be sold unlimited number of times. Online training program can accommodate thousands of participants to log in and use the training at the same time. Today's technology has developed so well that it can support hundreds of thousands of people across the world to access information seamlessly.

Some marketers apply the scarcity principle even to online broadcast events like webinars. *Only 200 people can participate. Open only for the first 500 people who login in.* All this is nonsense. Today, using Google Hangout, anyone can broadcast their webinar or event, LIVE to virtually an unlimited number of people all over the world. The technology is so developed and inexpensive that anyone can practically do a LIVE broadcast of any event with just a computer and an Internet connection.

So, when you see this scarcity tactic in any promotional material that you come across, pause for a moment and think whether the offer is really scarce enough that you need to act immediately.

DISCOUNTS

This is another tactic that creates a lot of hype and urgency to buy from unsuspecting prospects.

Discount is a psychological hot button that marketers have effectively used over centuries to make people buy their stuff right now, instead of thinking about it later.

By offering discounts, marketers sell more stuff in less time. This tactic is extremely good for... well, marketers. It puts more money into their pockets.

Discounts only make sense when the item offered has been sold or will surely be sold at a price that is higher than offered, ever. This means if any product has never been sold at a price that is higher than the discounted price, it is just a tactic and not true or ethical.

For example, if a product, let's say an online home-study program, is offered for $2,000 as the list price. The owner offers a discount of $1,000 (50% off) for everyone, then, it is a 'hype' tactic. If nobody has paid the full price for the product, it means the retail price is artificially inflated and a discount is applied just to make more sales.

Fear of losing something is a more powerful psychological trigger than the pleasure of gaining something. So marketers use this 'hype' tactic into tricking people to buy soon and buy more than they need.

To say that a discount is genuine, it must be proved that the product has already been sold at a higher price either in the past or will definitely be sold at a higher price in the near, verifiable future, like in cases of 'introductory-discounts'.

Large corporations often use discounts or coupons to get access into a new market, launch a new product or claim more market share for their products or services.

When I was in school I remember this new newspaper that started. That was the time when real newspapers were distributed to all homes, early in the morning. This new company didn't have any market share in the region, so, they started a campaign to go to every home in town and offered a free copy of their newspaper for 2 full months. That's a 100% discount for 2 consecutive months to try their product. It worked like a charm. If they had tried to ask their buyers to switch to their newspaper, they would have failed miserably. They offered a deep discount and took away all the risks of buying their product. Within no time the new newspaper's market share went from zero to 75%. Within months, all other local newspapers were out of business.

So, offering discounts is not new. Sometimes it is genuine, and most of the times, especially in the Internet Marketing world, it isn't. If something is offered at a discounted price, make sure to find out the actual price or the real price of the product before you feel good about the discount.

THE TRUTH ABOUT OUTSOURCING

There is a lot of confusion on exactly how the outsourcing model works, especially in the Internet Marketing industry.

Let me clear them up for you. I know this because we have fulfilled IM related services to hundreds of marketing companies all over the world.

Outsourcing isn't a bad idea, after all. If implemented correctly it can save money or time or both, and at the same time provide access to remote resources that were unavailable earlier. It can bring in talent and access to skills from anywhere in the world.

In the wrong hands (unethical marketers) it can become disastrous. Instead of driving the costs down, it may lead to getting short changed in terms of quality or quantity or both.

Especially in the online marketing and SEO industry, there are very few players that have their own staff for rendering services. Most have found someone in a developing country to fulfil. And, unfortunately, most marketers do not do their due-diligence to find the right fulfilment partner, or they go for the cheapest service provider.

You get what you pay for. That's what happens in this case too. Marketers charge premium prices from their clients and pass on the work on 'white-label' to their fulfilment partners in a remote corner of the world. They pay them peanuts and everybody knows what they get for peanuts – monkeys!

In such cases, there are two winners and a loser. The fulfilment partner gets a small piece of the deal, but that's good money because a dollar goes a long way in a developing country. They are happy. The marketer who makes the sale gobbles up the biggest chunk and wins too. The biggest loser is the chap who avails the services from such marketers. They pay top dollars thinking they are supporting a local business while they are getting cheap stuff from an untrained service provider in a different country.

They could have saved all the money by directly going to the actual service provider because technology today makes it possible to do business anywhere in the world. Alternatively, they could have paid top-dollars and got premium services for every penny they paid by dealing with a legitimate and ethical service provider, no matter where they are located.

At **infoYOGIS**, a big part of our revenue used to come from fulfilling Internet Marketing services to others companies. I have seen this happen many times in the past. The marketer or a self-proclaimed GURU would first contact us, make connection, promise bulk orders and get us to sign a contract for ultra-low prices. Then he would go back and build a business around this contract, crank up the prices 8 to 10 times, add nothing in value for the increased price and sell our services at a premium price. It is the same stuff we used to sell on our website, but 10 times more expensive. Today, with our presence in the market and offices worldwide, our services are available to our clients directly, at reasonable prices and world-class quality.

FREE... REALLY!?

The word FREE is one of most used and abused word in the history of marketing. The word 'free' is powerful and a psychological hot button that is used by marketers for centuries. It also connects people to the word 'freedom' that resonates with human beings being free to control or obligation or will of another, like in political freedom.

Giving something away for free makes sense only if that 'something' is of value to the recipient. Most marketers do not get this correctly and offer useless stuff that nobody wants or they go a step further and implement this half-baked knowledge into their client's business as well.

Businesses and individuals hire marketers or marketing companies because they think they are experts in their field and let these experts manage their online marketing activities. Very dangerous. Not recommended at all. Marketing or branding is an important part of any individual or business and must be dealt with by trained professionals only. Just like you go to a doctor when your body needs surgery, you go to an architect to construct buildings. Similarly, you need a real and experienced marketing expert to take care of your online marketing needs.

If someone offers you anything for free, or if YOU are offering anything for free on your website, it is time to pause and look at whether the free stuff offered is useful and valuable. Does it help? Does it make any sense? If yes, continue. Otherwise, stop the nonsense and think of offering something else for free-genuinely.

There are many things that marketers offer for free including free reports, eBooks, software, free bonuses for buying the products they recommend and so on. It is not wrong to offer something for free. However, just make sure the value still exists, even though the price is set to zero.

For example, at **infoYOGIS**, we offer a free online business assessment for people who need online marketing help. This report is actually put together by a team of people. They spend hours to research and collate the data and put together a report that is full of useful content that the recipient can actually use in their business.

I also do regular Google Hangouts on Air and broadcast my talk all over the world on topics like "Stardom Strategies," for example. These are strictly "no-sales" webinars. There won't be anything to offer at the end of these webinars. They are full of valuable content and offered for free. The only purpose of such events is to educate my audience. Teach them, train them and to an extent, entertain them. That's all. My members LOVE those hangouts because they get valuable information that they can use in their lives right away!

The best way to offer something for free is to create a product (or a service), fix a price, sell a few copies and THEN offer it for free. That's a really free offer.

HYPE TRIGGERS

Here are some words that I call as hype-triggers. When I see those words or phrases, my hype-guard goes up. Unscrupulous marketers and scammers use these heavily to push their stuff. When you see such words in emails, offers and announcements, pause for a moment and do a thorough reality-check before proceeding:

- **Expert** – Used widely. I wonder how anyone can become an expert in days while people who have devoted their lifetime or decades of their life still don't consider themselves as experts!
- **Secret** – Ah... the classic hype trigger word. Today, everyone seems to have a secret. Watch out for this. Making a lot of rounds, especially in the Internet Marketing circles.
- **Traffic** – Essentially means website traffic. Unethical marketers are selling packages that promise website visitors and delivering crap.

- **First Page Rankings** – Another classic hype. Nobody can promise first page rankings without first evaluating the keywords. Even then, if anyone offers first-page rankings, look with suspicion.

Other common marketing hype trigger words include solution, push-button effort, at the touch of a button, backdoor entry (yes, used to trick people into believing there are such hidden methods for otherwise hard strategies), confidential report, winning or lottery related, free giveaways, etc. Feel free to add to this list other hype-triggers that you come across.

About Raam Anand

Raam Anand is the founder of infoYOGIS, Asia's LARGEST Internet Marketing agency. He is also the founder of Stardom Alliance, which helps people achieve stardom and become one of the most sought-after authorities in their fields. Raam started "TheSpeakingTree.org" - a movement against unethical marketing.

Raam was involved in systems programming to some of the leading banks and financial institutions in core areas like online banking, ATM interface, asset management, online transaction processing, inter-branch networking and so on.

Since 1992, Raam has served in leading positions like Technical Director of PSL, Managing Director of Tempus Data Services, and CEO of infoYOGIS, besides being an active adviser to several leading financial institutions and marketing companies.

Raam stepped into Internet Marketing in 2001 and since then he has published several highly successful software programs and products. His home study course - "Site Launch System" received a lot of praise and started a new market in the industry that many other people followed. His next training program "AgencyRiches" was responsible for helping many of his students start and run their own profitable IM agencies.

Raam started his own Internet Marketing agency in 2006 called infoYOGIS. Under his leadership and vision, this company soon grew from a 1-man operation to a 100+ people organization in 3 years and went on to become the LARGEST Internet Marketing Agency in Asia.

Raam has more than a decade of experience in the IM industry and is one of the pioneers of online marketing. He has toured the world several times, visited more than 15 countries and speaks often at seminars and conferences all over the world. He also conducts workshops, boot camps and mastermind sessions. As the CEO of infoYOGIS, he also provides consulting services for large companies throughout the world.

Other than being a sought-after coach, thoughtful trainer and a well-known business leader who is ardently followed and admired by his students, Raam is also serving as the managing trustee of a non-profit institution, engaged in charity, education and research.

Get more details, additional training, download and access his videos by visiting Raam Anand's personal website at www.RaamAnand.com

"For a truly effective social campaign, a brand needs to embrace the first principles of marketing, which involves brand definition and consistent storytelling."

~Simon Mainwaring~

Chapter 7

From Guru Wannabe to African Internet Visioneer

The Success Secrets I Learned From The Gurus and How It Can Help You Succeed Too!

By Dr. Ope Banwo

It was June 2012 when it happened.

I was a successful attorney, (with a practice in Omaha, Nebraska and Lagos, Nigeria) who also owned a record label, an entertainment management company and a host of other business ventures.

On that day, I was lazily browsing the internet trying to kill some time between business meetings when I came upon a random email talking about the *"Coffee Shop Millionaire."* What the hell is the *"Coffee Shop Millionaire?"* I thought to myself as I clicked the email open.

That Was How I Discovered Internet marketing.

But first let me tell you a little bit about myself. I am a very successful Attorney here in Omaha, Nebraska and I run several companies in the USA and my native Nigeria.

I was NOT broke and I was NOT desperate at the time I chose to become an internet marketer. I was not only making a good income, I actually was paying (and still do) more than 30 staff members in my various businesses every month.

So why did the "make money online" bug bite me?
I'll Tell You Why...

For as long as I can remember, I've always been a sucker for starting businesses, new businesses, and making them widely profitable.

When I saw that email in my inbox about the coffee shop millionaire, I caught the bug.

I just had to start my own internet company, not really for the money, but at least for the thrill and ego of succeeding in yet another business field.

And Down I Went Down The Rabbit Hole...

In a little over six months, after I read the "Coffee Shop" millionaire email, *I bought over 200 eBooks, software and coaching from Warrior Forum, over 100 from JV Zoo and another 50+ from Clickbank in less than 6 months!*

If that sounds astonishing, it isn't. For many newbies, it is reality. Most have maxed out their credit cards and overextended their checking accounts so much that they are either in or near bankruptcy, just to realize their internet marketing dream.

And have so far failed.

For me, it wasn't about the money, per se. It was the thought that I couldn't get this to work, the thought that I had let down myself.

For the first time in my life, I saw defeat staring me right in the face.

But I Was No Quitter!

I continued learning, experimenting, meeting new folks and implementing like a mad man.

Things started changing very fast. I started seeing success.

I had my first $3,000 month online. Then, I had my first $20,000 month (a 650% increase in revenue by the way) and now approaching $100,000 a month!

Since then I have pulled in several hundreds of thousands of dollars from my online efforts and have been brought in as a board member in a couple of companies to advise them on their internet marketing strategies.

So how did I go from a bumbling internet marketing fortune seeker who was clueless for over 12 months, to finally cracking the success code and then rising to the top in less than 6 months after figuring it out?

For the answer to that $100,000 question, I will like to share some of the secrets I learned from the Gurus during my journey in wannabe land:

- **Breakthrough Guru Discovery #1**
  Real Gurus Have A Strategic Focus To Their Internet Business
  The most important secret I learned from the gurus in my eventful journey as a guru wannabe was that I needed to have a strategic focus for my business. This is way deeper than the traditional thinking that what you need to succeed is to find a hungry niche and service that hunger. It even goes beyond just writing a business plan for your business.

  This secret is knowing what you want, where you want to be, examining the options open to you to get there, and determining the best option that will get you there, with the least amount of resistance and competition.

I learned from the gurus that just finding a hungry niche is no longer enough. You cannot be successful in the long run, without working yourself to death, by simply servicing a niche. You have to have an overriding strategy that guides everything you do online.

This is a profound revelation that is critical to your future in internet marketing and you need to grasp it before you can move forward.

I discovered that having an internet marketing strategy is not about what you are doing, but how you are THINKING. In other words, whether you are an opportunity seeker or a strategic entrepreneur is determined by how you think about yourself and your business.

- **Breakthrough Discovery #2**
  Real Gurus Outsource Most Tasks In their Businesses
  While locked up in my basement doing my self-imposed Internet Marketing Rehab, I did a thorough investigation of the other things that made the gurus special, other than having a clear strategy.

I discovered that, without any exception, they were all masters of strategic outsourcing.
The real gurus, who were eating the lunches of the guru wannabes like me, right from under our noses, every day, tended to outsource most tasks in their businesses, including some tasks they could do by themselves!

While floundering around as a guru wannabe, I had been

practically doing everything myself. I did my own keyword research and designed and created my own products; I handled the traffic generation; forum posting; list building; accounting and many other functions that I erroneously believed needed to be handled personally by me. About the only thing I outsourced were the graphic designs for my book products and my website sales pages.

In my mind, I thought I was supposed to outsource only those things I could not do myself. I foolishly believed that by doing most of the things I was capable of doing I was saving myself some money. Yet the need for outsourcing in my business has nothing to do with my capability, or otherwise, to do a task! A careful study of the approach of the real gurus to outsourcing in their businesses showed that it has nothing to do with what they can do or cannot do themselves.

Rather, for the gurus, the decision to outsource, or not outsource, has everything to do with the *value* of the gurus time and whether the gurus can get someone to do the task at a rate lower than their time was worth.

It was a paradigm shift of colossal proportions.

All I can tell you right here is that understanding what my time is really worth, combined with an understanding of how proper outsourcing really works, has been a major boost to my internet business.

Now, I work less while earning more. I am no longer as stressed as I used to be and yet, there is a major improvement in my income. I was actually able to set up a whole internet business school, in less than 2 weeks, spending less than 2 hours a day on it. It was amazing.

- **Breakthrough Guru Secret #3**
Real Gurus Maximize the Power of Leverage By Developing Most Of Their Products Around One Niche
Contrary to my own opportunistic, knee jerk approach to creating products as a guru wannabe, I discovered that the real gurus actually focus tightly on one niche for a long time. The real gurus take time to design their long term strategy for their business, which also invariably include finding the niche they want to dominate, and how to dominate it over the long term.

Once they have done that, they then use their considerable resources to build a full complement of products, email follow-ups, one time offers (OTO) and upsells in that one niche, which they then market to their list and the market at large relentlessly.

When you take a look at the products created by some of the acknowledged gurus, such as Brad Fallon, Mike Filsaime, Rich Schefren, Alex Jeffreys and Matt Bacak, you will observe that each of them focused on only one niche!

They always make sure everything they are doing in internet marketing is tightly connected with the niche they are operating in. They do not just promote or buy anything simply because it is hot. It has to be tied to their niche or they will pass on it, no matter how juicy.

Most guru wannabes like me, who did not really have a strategic vision, on the other hand, simply jump from one niche to the other in pursuit of easy money. At the end of the day, they have no leverage, as they are not building on the strength of their past affiliates and customer bases.

- **Breakthrough Guru Secret #4**
Real Gurus Aggressively Develop an Army of JV Partners to Help With Their Product Launches
Another major discovery in my wandering around as a guru wannabe is the realization that virtually all the major gurus have an impressive army of affiliates and JV Partners on call at all times. I found out that, apart from developing great products several times a year, gurus spend most of their time cultivating and developing relationships with JV Partners and super affiliates.

In my early days as a guru-wannabe, I just assumed that affiliates would review your offer on JVzoo or Warrior plus or Clickbank and then make a decision whether to promote your product or not. I naively thought that the strength or utility of a product was the major thing that determined whether it would be promoted or not. However, I quickly found out that this is not so.

As a matter of fact, the game is totally rigged against the newbie who has no clue.

Apparently, most gurus, many months BEFORE their product's release date, do a lot of backroom wheeling and dealing to recruit powerful affiliates and JV Partners to promote their product and give it a big bounce on opening day. There really is nothing accidental or fair about how the gurus get big gravity scores on ClickBank or high EPCs on opening day of their product launch.

The gurus who are having those 6 and 7 figure launches you keep hearing about on a regular basis often focus a lot more time on getting JV's and affiliates for the product launch than they spend creating the product itself.

So, I learned from watching the masters do their thing that to be a real guru in this business, it is imperative that you learn and master how to gather JV's and get willing affiliates to promote your products. Statistics, from those who should know, actually claim that over 80% of most sales were done by JVs and affiliates. So, you must learn how to attract JV's and Affiliates, or get buried. It's that simple.

- **Breakthrough Guru Secret #5**
  Real Gurus Understand the Power of Networking Events
  If you have ever wondered how the gurus always seem to manage to put together an intimidating army of loyalists and affiliates to promote their products, the answer is really very simple: Internet Marketing Events!

Contrary to what most guru-wannabes think, these affiliates and JV partners do not appear from thin air, and they are not sourced by spamming on Facebook or through adverts. The super gurus get these army of affiliates by attending and networking with people at Internet Marketing Events. Though it took me a while to figure this out, I finally realized that you can accelerate your progress in the Internet Marketing world by attending Internet Marketing events as often as you can.

As a matter of fact, I will venture to suggest that if you can attend 3 - 5 Internet Marketing events a year, you are bound to be connected with super hitters within your first year that would help you to make serious money in this business, regardless of where you are right now.

Ordinarily, many of these guys will not give you the time of day in another setting. They will not respond to your emails and will more likely than not embarrass you if you tried to approach them on social media or elsewhere about supporting your project if you were not in their inner circle. However, catch them at an Internet Marketing event and they will treat you like an equal or a long lost friend. People who would ordinarily charge you $5,000 just to speak to you for one hour will drink with you all night and share amazing secrets of the trade with you at a costume party. This was really an incredible revelation to me personally!

I can honestly tell you that if you have not been attending events, you are missing the most powerful single weapon to get access to these busy and sometimes inaccessible heavyweights.

It is my hope that you have learned a thing or two from these secrets. My journey to breaking the barriers to succeed in Internet Marketing was not pretty, but I was able to find a ray of sunlight at the end of the tunnel, through sheer perseverance and unyielding tenacity.

Payday To Playday

About Dr. Ope Banwo

Dr. Ope Banwo, has a Ph.d in Law, is an Entrepreneur, Attorney, Motivational Speaker and Internet Business Consultant.

Dr. Ope Banwo is a gifted Speaker and Writer who has published several books on Personal Development, Business, Internet Marketing and Christian lifestyle. He is the author of books including Overcoming The Gideon Complex; The Blessings of Adversity; Confessions of a Guru Wannabe; and African Internet Business Manifesto and The Kingdom Citizen. He has created several internet business products such as LinkedIn Marketing Miracle; FB Marketing Miracle;

Dr. Ope Banwo strongly believes it is the duty of everyone to maximize their God-Given Talents in any area or industry they are gifted or positioned to be of help to others. His personal mission is to apply his talents, skills and training to help as many people and businesses as possible to find solutions to their problems regardless of their industry.

He is passionate social responsibility and believes that service to humanity is the greatest work of life. Dr. Ope Banwo is the founder of several charity organizations including Ghetto Dreamz Foundation; The Market Ombudsman and The Election Vigilantes International.

He is currently the Chief Executive, Afrinet Business Solutions Inc.; Managing Partner at Banwo and Igbokwe, LLC and Executive Director at American Internet Business School.

He is married with 4 children and has homes in Omaha, Nebraska USA and Lagos, Nigeria

Check out Dr. Ope at **www.OpeBanwo.com.**

"Busiess has only two functions - marketing and innovation."

~Milan Kundera ~

Chapter 8

Building Online Business Relationships
Six Steps to building a stronger, more profitable business
By Dennis Hall

If you're reading this, I'm betting that you fall into one (or more) of three categories:

1. You are looking for some insights on how to create a successful online business or,
2. You want to build on the success of an existing online business or,
3. You want to help offline businesses make better use of their internet potential

No matter what category you fall into, I am going to show you how to improve the results of ANY business – online or offline - dealing direct with the public (B2C) or with other businesses (B2B).

Firstly, let me make one thing abundantly clear – if you are looking for that "Magic" formula that guarantees success (and, let's face it, it's tempting to believe in a "Silver bullet" that fixes everything, makes life simple and generates bucket loads of money!) – I'm going to disappoint you.

Magic formulas, silver bullets, mystical secrets and the like are the stuff of fairy tales and, in the broader business world, we know deep down that fairy tales aren't real. Mind you, that doesn't stop thousands of people from continuing to live in fairyland!

So let's dispense with the fairy tales. Whether you want to build your business or help others to build theirs, there are no guarantees to success, and no fairy tales that will result in it either!

But there is definitely a difference between the things successful businesspeople do, as opposed to those that are unsuccessful. One of those things is their approach to how they establish, build and value relationships. Whether you are looking to create an online empire or leverage the online environment to boost your offline business, you are going to need to be able to build effective business relationships that deliver value.

Business has always been about relationships – not the kind we are used to with our friends or families, but the kind of relationships that are built on a platform of mutual understanding, respect and exchange. The exchange part is what most people focus on – this is where the customer exchanges money (or other acceptable trading currency) for the solutions that the business they are dealing with is providing them.

In reality, the exchange is just the tip of the relationship iceberg – it's what is most visible – but there's a whole lot more going on here than simply an exchange. There's communication in establishing needs & conveying solutions, there's building rapport and trust, and there's establishment of respect.

No matter what platform you conduct your business through – online or offline – these relationship steps are present and, if you get it right, you have the makings of a successful business at hand.

Yes, there are a lot of other ingredients that will contribute to the profitability and success of a business, but ultimately, getting the relationship component right will smooth over a lot of rough edges and will definitely improve your position against competitors.

We're not here to go through those other success factors, we're here to nail the relationship aspect – so let's get to it!

By now you're starting to wonder what all of this has to do with the internet and online marketing – so here it is – the way we do business may be changing, thanks to the internet, but the core tenets of business are not. To be successful in business you need a solid business model, thorough planning and a passion to make a difference. Technology has to be viewed as a tool to improve a business, to paraphrase a famous quote on money – "Technology is an awesome servant but a tyrannical master."

What the internet does better than any other business tool is enable you to communicate with huge numbers of people at extremely low cost. That is both an advantage and a disadvantage.

It's an advantage because the cost to acquire new customers and retain existing ones is reduced.

It's a disadvantage because if you get things wrong, everyone finds out really quickly!

In the days before the internet, the damage caused through some "Trial and Error" processes to getting your business model right, could be contained fairly easily and dealt with. Today, a "Hiccup" in one market segment can be the downfall of the entire business – YouTube is littered with videos that have gone viral based on a business getting it wrong. Funny to view – unless it's your business and you find you've lost most of your customers overnight.

The major game changer though, is that the internet has shifted the balance of power in trading relationships from the supplier to the consumer. When a customer is online they are, literally, just one click away from your competitors.

So, in that environment – how do you stop them from making that click or, if they do click – how do you get them to click back to you?

It all gets down to the strength of the relationship. You have to shift focus to building that relationship – through understanding their needs, communicating that understanding through your value proposition(s), and making your messages personal to them – you concentrate on interaction, on generating a conversation, because that builds rapport, which leads to higher levels of trust.

If you don't do this, you end up focusing on the transaction (the exchange) & when you do that you force your customer to evaluate you on just one thing – price. In an online savvy world that's a recipe for the "One click away" behaviour where you only get the business if you're the cheapest – that's not a healthy place to be, as it puts enormous pressure on your margins and business viability.

So, how do you build better business relationships? How do you move away from a focus on transactions to an emphasis on interaction & engagement?

Here is my six step process:

1. **Who do you want a relationship with?**
The most common error I see people in business making is that they believe that anyone with a dollar to spend is a

potential customer. This is a big mistake!

Strong relationships are built on understanding. If you go after everyone, how can you hope to understand them all, let alone get them to understand you?

This "One size fits all" model no longer works and hasn't for decades. The 20th Century business imperative was to appeal to the "Mass market" – that's where the profits were. Today, thanks to the internet, we have "Masses of markets" with people (that's you, me and everyone else), looking for businesses that understand them.

People no longer want to be just a "Number" (as was the case in a "Mass market" world), they want (& in many cases demand) to be treated as an individual.

Simply put, you need to "Personalise" your communications with your customers to represent a part of their solution – if you don't, then they will see you as a part of their problem! When you narrow down your target customer group(s) to the smallest commercially viable number, these "Personal" conversations are far easier.

One way to identify your target groups is to ask yourself: "Who would benefit most from using this (& why)?" (If you already have a product/service to deliver). Or; "Who would I like to do business with (&why)?" (If you don't yet have a product/service).

Then ask, "What problems (of theirs) are you suited to solving?

I have developed an "Ideal customer" profiling tool that

shows just how this can be done – email me if you would like one!

2. What do you need to know about them?

It's time to get personal! To build better business relationships you need to know your customer's needs, you need to understand their world, and you need to be able to communicate to them in the ways they require (not in the ways that are easiest for you).

Develop a customer profile that describes the type of customer(s) you are seeking to develop relationships with – what is their age group/gender? Where do they live? What does their world look like? What problems do they face (& need solutions for)? What is their income?

The more detailed your profile is, the better able you will be to establish meaningful relationships with people fitting that profile. Don't worry if you don't have answers to all of your profile questions – the questions you are missing answers to become a part of your communications strategy to get to know them better (after you have established contact).

3. What are your touch points?

Knowing where your potential customers tend to gather provides you with an idea of the sorts of environments you will need to deal with when communicating to your customers and potential customers. I refer to these environments as "Touch points"

Do you want to communicate with them whilst they are at work, at home, at play – or a combination of these (& other) touch points?

Understanding where someone is when they are exposed to you and your messages is crucial in building high trust relationships that are relevant and perceived as being of value.

4. What conversations do you intend having?

Relationships are built through a process of interactions (as opposed to sales which are merely transactions). These interactions are best viewed as a series of conversations – not necessarily vocal communication but any interaction between you and your customers and potential customers.

What conversations you will have, and when, will be decided by your relationship timeline and the status of the customer. For example, existing customers are looking for different conversations to those of potential customers.

With your relationship timeline you need to understand the process that your ideal customers go through when making buying decisions and tailor your conversations to suit that timeline. My "Next Step" relationship building program is based on this concept and provides businesspeople with a methodology that can be applied to any business model (you can email me to get a free copy if you wish).

The difference between what someone considers being "Junk" and relevant is in what the content (of the communication) is about and the timing of delivery. When you truly understand your customers, and potential customers, you significantly lessen the risk of your conversations being seen as an "Intrusion" or "Junk."

5. What mechanisms will you employ?

Knowing what conversation to have and when to have them is one thing, but utilising the most relevant mechanisms is another. Here is where too many businesses fail the relationship test – they engage mechanisms that suit them more than their customers.

In the 20th Century, businesses justified this approach on the basis of cost – tailoring the content of a message and personalising the delivery mechanism was simply too expensive. To an extent, this was true, but the internet has changed all of that – and your customers know it!

Outside of the email solution, there are numerous online mechanisms open to you today – Social media (Facebook, Twitter, Linked in, etc.), Mobile (SMS, Apps, QR codes, etc.), Video (YouTube, Vimeo, etc.), Blogs, Interactive websites. The list is almost endless!

However, whilst the number of available mechanisms can be intimidating, making a choice on which to employ is a lot more straightforward when you are able to answer the question, "Which of these (mechanisms) does my ideal customer utilise (or appreciate) most?"

6. What's my feedback loop?
You can't build better business relationships without listening to what your customers and potential customers have to say about what you are (or are not) doing.

How will you provide your customers with the opportunity to let you know how you're doing? Additionally, are you listening to what they're saying about you unofficially (to their friends, family and colleagues)?

More importantly, how will you make sure that your response to that feedback is both relevant & timely?

Here's where Social media, Blogs (review sites and the like) & online surveys really come into their own!

If all of this seems like hard work – you're right! Building better business relationships online is hard work – but done right, it is what will separate your business from most of the rest.

And here's the really interesting part – customers who feel valued and understood appreciate the effort that has been made to achieve that (yes, they know you've made the effort!) and they will reward you in two ways:

1. They'll resist competitor approaches, be less price sensitive and;
2. They'll tell their friends about you!

Now, that second part is the most interesting and it's where the internet really comes into its own. For most of the 20th Century, word of mouth recommendation was seen as being powerful but limited – it was estimated that most people's circle of influence was 7-10 people.

The internet has significantly widened that circle – for example, Facebook users, on average, have 100 "Friends." So, if you have a strong relationship with a customer and they post that on their timeline (there are programs to assist you encourage that to happen as a part of your feedback loop), 100 people see it – more importantly, as soon as any of those "Friends" comment on or like that post, their 100 "Friends" see that! In no time at all thousands of people have been introduced to your business, based on a recommendation from someone they know, and that's far more powerful than an advertisement!

It's the old "Multiplier" effect – two tell two, four tell four, eight tell eight and so on – in no time flat your business growth booms!

Don't forget, though, that this multiplier effect is also in play if your customer feels you have let them down!

Yes, I know that the temptation to take the easy path is there – go for volume, blast out the numbers & tell everyone you possibly can the same message. Then rinse and repeat for the next "New thing."

I'm not suggesting you can't make money doing that – you can. But at what cost in the long term? The internet is evolving - fast! We already have email SPAM laws and there are moves for regulation to bolster privacy laws, etc.

You can stay one jump ahead of the regulators and still make money. For me, though, I'd much rather build a business that people grow to respect and that my customers value, because that will have far more longevity and, not only will I make money but I will be proud of what I've achieved.

How about you?

Payday To Playday

About Dennis Hall
The Communication Commando

Dennis has an extensive corporate marketing background which spans more than 35 years in the private sector, in industries including electronics, consumer goods, publishing, tourism, hospitality and Information Technology.

In 1997 Dennis gave up his corporate life as Director of Marketing & Sales in a multi-million dollar Hotel & Resort company to start his own business focused on assisting small businesses deal with the looming threat of the Y2k "Millennium Bug." This quickly evolved into providing Information Technology (I.T.) infrastructure support.

As the business grew, Dennis realised that his real passion was in applying his marketing expertise to provide small businesses and enterprises with support to realise their potential through leveraging the growing power of the internet. This mirrored the increasing amount of questions he was getting from his clients along the lines of, "How can I get the internet to work for my business?"

So, in 2003, he sold the I.T. component of the business to focus on Internet Marketing for offline businesses – more than 6 years before the term "Offline business" became more commonly applied!

This involved a steep learning curve as, whilst he was a seasoned marketer, online marketing technologies were new to him (and most of the rest of the world). Fortunately, fate stepped in and Dennis met a person who was to become a guiding force for him in coming to understand these technologies – as well as a close personal friend. That person was David Cavanagh, soon to be a world renowned authority on starting and building online businesses.

That chance meeting resulted in Dennis being introduced to many of the leading lights involved in the cutting edge of Internet Marketing such as, Alex Mendossian, Armand Morin, Stephen Pierce, Brett McFall, Mitch Carson, Robert Plank and many more.

These days Dennis regularly speaks at conferences throughout Australia & South East Asia on the subjects of "Building better business relationships," "Generational diversity," "Personal productivity in business," "Putting customers first" and "Web2.0 marketing," while also providing training to businesspeople in the corporate arena on building better business relationships – both internally & externally.

He has developed a series of online programs designed to help offline businesses harness the power of the online world. The centerpiece of these being his "Next Step" online relationship building program.

This program, and many of his other programs, serve to bring together proven marketing principles, as well as to "De-mystify" the mechanics of the internet and, in so doing, provide businesspeople with clarity on what they need to be doing to leverage the online environment for their advantage. He is continually "Fine tuning" his programs so as to ensure that emerging online trends and technologies are taken advantage of.

His services are in high demand, with high profile Australian organisations such as Hastings Deering, Suncorp Banking Group, AECOM and Sunshine Coast University being just a few of his recent clients. He is a registered Coach and Facilitator with the Australian Institute of Management, a Fellow for the Institute of Learning Practitioners and holds an MBA in marketing management.

He lives with his wife and youngest daughter in Australia, based in Noosa on Queensland's Sunshine Coast.

Dennis can be contacted via email at **dennis@denishall.com.au.**

"In marketing I've seen only one strategy that can't miss - and that is to market to your best customers first, your best prospects second and the rest of the world last."

~John Romero ~

Chapter 9

Building Wealth Through Real Estate

By Tim & Janelle Johnson

Real Estate investing is one of the best ways to build up wealth.

There will always be businesses that will thrive in their season, and there are others that will thrive for the moment. Like everything else, there is a rise and fall in the real estate market in general. Even with that, you can still benefit from real estate investing. In fact, when the economy is *not* at its greatest, this becomes some of the best times for potential real estate investors to get great deals for investment properties.

When the prices of properties are lower, banks want to sell quickly. Another possible aspect about a sluggish market is that you still have some stability, even with a downturn in the economy. Don't think that when there are economic downturns, that it is the end of the world. It isn't. People don't realize that it is one of the best times to purchase property at an affordable price.

For those who are interested in real estate investing, this can be a great deal for those who can get in the market quickly to snatch up those homes and use them as rental properties. You just have to make sure that you are in the right place at the right time.

Generating Positive Cash Flow

When looking at real estate properties as financial investments, you will have to decide whether an appreciated value or positive cash flow is your main goal for buying properties. Before you can make that decision, there are a few things that you will need to consider.

81

Since you would probably be looking at both single family homes and multifamily homes, note that there is a difference between the two. With the former, the value of the property usually increases in value quicker. However, since more expenses are attached, you may not be looking at the kind of positive cash flow that you want.

On the other hand, multifamily units (i.e., duplexes), can generate more positive cash flow. But, they may not appreciate quickly like single-family homes do, and there may not be as many expenses attached to the latter. Since most real estate investors look to create wealth, they will most likely choose having a positive cash flow. In this case, you will need a reliable real estate agent that is willing to help you find real estate properties that will produce the positive cash flow that you want.

Real Estate Investing Tips

I can't stress enough the fact that when you're starting out, don't rush into getting the first piece of property that you see. It's important that you conduct your due diligence. Even though it is a lucrative and profitable business, you can lose money if you don't work it properly. Look at the balance sheets and see what you will look forward to as far as repairs, maintenance, fees and other miscellaneous expenses.

Don't listen to all of those stories that you hear about people making lots of money "overnight" with real estate investing. It can take weeks or months to actually get the property that you want, and it takes more than a day to start seeing a profit.

If you take your time and look around, you may be surprised as to how much is available to you in terms of real estate properties. There seems to never be a shortage of places where you can find a place to use for a profitable investment. But find a good real estate agent that is willing to genuinely help you. You may even be fortunate enough to find one that is also an investor on the side.

Now once you get into real estate investing, it's very important to stay in it for the long haul. That's the way you will create wealth. There are those who like getting their feet wet when the iron is hot, but when it gets cold, they want to bail out. Regardless of whether the market is up or down, you must be willing to weather any storms that come about.

Gaining lucrative wealth from real estate investing comes with staying the course. Let's take a look at some of the ways that can help you make real estate investing worthwhile:

- ❖ When you do decide to purchase property for investing purposes, seek counsel from those who have come before you. It's important that you have adequate information before you jump into something like this. Real estate investing involves time and money. You need both in order to make this business work for you, and you not working for it.
- ❖ Find experienced investors that are willing to spend time showing you some of the ins and outs of real estate investing. They can share some of their experiences with you and advise you on what to look out for.
- ❖ Try not to hoard a bunch of properties all at once. Start out with one and then work your way up. Working at a slower pace will help you to properly maintain and manage what you have.
- ❖ Having adequate knowledge prior to making the leap into a venture like this can help you avoid the pitfalls that can

befall some new real estate investors. Getting into real estate investing can be exciting and lucrative, but you have to be willing to deal with the negatives as well as the positives.

❖ Have realistic goals and remember that real estate investing is a process. Those who claimed to have gotten their wealth quickly through real estate investing probably don't have it now.

❖ Even in downtimes, you can still profit. There will always be people that are looking for a place to live.

❖ After you feel comfortable with the first one, then you may want to look for the next one, and so on. This will help you to appreciate your investments better as opposed to being in a hurry to make money and acquire wealth.

❖ Getting the right tenant for your properties can sometimes be a hassle. However, it's better to take your time and get the right people so you can avoid a major headache later.

❖ It takes a lot to maintain and manage real estate properties. When you get to the point where you have a nice cash flow every month, you can hire a property management company to do the work for you. This will free you from the tasks that you would get used to doing yourself. That would include getting rental payments and dealing with various tenant issues.

❖ Since you are not Superman, don't expect to do all of the repairs yourself. There may be some minor cosmetic issues you can take care of. Other than that, leave it up to the professionals.

❖ In addition to repairs, you will need to keep enough funds on hand in order to honor your mortgage loan obligations on time.

❖ Try to keep an open mind and don't get yourself worked up when things go wrong, as they will when you have tenants. If you do your homework, you can avoid some of the issues that can happen to investors.

❖ You will be able to increase rent as time goes on. This will help you produce a cash surplus while you are still paying the same amount on your mortgage loan. This of course, can happen if you have a structured loan payment that doesn't fluctuate during any given period.

❖ Be better than your competition. Don't just put up a sign and hope that people will come. You have to market and advertise. You may need to place ads in the paper and get with seasoned real estate professionals to help you.

❖ Eventually you will have so many investment properties that you won't have a choice but to hire a property management company to take over. Of course, you will have to set aside funds to pay them for their services. That's all the more reason for you to take it easy when it comes to building wealth with real estate investments.

You will be successful once you employ strategies that take you from one step to the next. It's better to have properties that will provide you with a steady income rather than waiting on the next blockbuster that may take years to come.

Payday To Playday

About The Authors

Business owner, entrepreneur, philanthropist, husband and father, Tim Johnson started his first company at the age of 24, which included designing a new product and acquiring investment capital necessary to finance the company's operations. Shortly thereafter he started his next company and eventually created enough capital to get him into the real estate business. He spent the next few years working with investors from all over the country, and he would share with these investors his methods of investing in real estate.

Tim has always been interested in real estate and real estate financing. In 2010 he started his own property management company, Bradley Management, LLC, which Janelle runs. This company grew very quickly and provides a variety of services to investors all over the world.

Tim is now involved with the development and growth of the exciting personal development and branding company called The Market Maker Group, LLC. Having created a considerable on line brand and professional presence, Tim realized every individual needs their own mark. Tim understands the importance of creating, maintaining and defending your reputation, and is dedicated to helping every individual meet those needs.

Bradley Management, LLC is an Indiana based company established in 2010 that helps investors throughout the world invest, renovate and manage real estate.

The company uses its personnel's vast experiences to provide a wide variety of services for its customers so that all their needs are met in the real estate market. Bradley Management has a reputation for meeting those needs and, therefore, the company has grown accordingly. The Market Maker Group provides an aid to businesses to help them reach their marketing goals.

For more information on Tim, Janelle and their services, check out
Yourpropertyresourcecenter.com
bradleymanagementgroup.com,

or contact Tim directly at
tim@bradleymanagementgroup.com.

"*Every single thing I learned about marketing and building my business, I learned from my mom, and she had never been in the workforce. She just had great practical sense.*"

~Barbara Corcoran~

Chapter 10

Take Your Own Rifle to the Shooting Gallery
Or, How To Pick Your **Real** Online Money-Making Business
From A Sea Of False Hope
by Rick Mortimer

So you've decided to embrace the greatest opportunity of the 21st Century, and start an online business? Outstanding choice!

Welcome to the 1%!

No, not *that* 1% -- reaching top income bracket status might be in your future, but it certainly will not happen overnight, or from simply making a decision.

The 1% we're referring to here is a different statistic: over **50%** of American adults dream of starting their own business someday. Less than **1%** actually make the decision to do so, and follow through.

It is not coincidence that the great majority of the top income earners entered that elite group as a direct result of a business startup, either by them or by a family member. Entrepreneurism is the time-tested route to wealth in America. But that route passes through dangerous territories, and it is littered with the remains of enterprises that never made it to the Promised Land.

The failure rates for new startups are high, and fear of failure, coupled with the need to raise seed capital are the main reasons that only 1 in 50 dreamers ever steps into the shoes of an action-taker. Whether a restaurant, a dry cleaners, a retail shop, or a professional practice, startup costs for nearly any business requiring a physical location are measured in six-figure multiples.

Costs are much more modest in the internet world, and opportunities abound. It has taken about 20 years for annual online sales to go from zero to $1 trillion; projections indicate that we will see the second trillion added to the annual figures by 2017 -- a doubling from 2013 rates in only 4 years.

So, **exactly how** will you get a piece of all the action? Where will you start, what direction will you choose, and what vehicle will you use? How can you hope to separate the real gems -- and there are many -- from the overwhelming crush of pure crap being hawked to aspiring online business owners today?

The marketplace for money making opportunities and products is very much like a gigantic carnival midway -- a largely unregulated shout-fest, though the FTC does try to keep sellers in line by occasionally taking action to show they're still watching.

Barkers and pitchmen have moved up the technology scale, but the idea too often remains the same -- separating you from your money as quickly and effortlessly as possible, with no regard to giving any real value in return.

We can offer a few crude rules of thumb for you to keep in mind as you wander around the carnie:

- The more appealing the offer sounds to the horde of newbies and wannabes, the more you should be seeing yellow flags waving. What is a "perfect" offer to the uninitiated?
    1) No cash requirement to get started, just buy "this"
    2) Zero technical skills required
    3) Extremely high income, very quickly

4) Almost no ongoing time or work required

5) Anyone can do it, no problem, easy as pie

- Your yellow flags should turn red immediately if these elements appear:

    1) **Multiple exit pops.** Before you hit the order button, try closing the offer window. If you get more than one or two *"Wait!! You're making the biggest mistake of your life!!"* type pop-up messages, you might be connected to an old-school spammer at heart. Remember the viruses that trapped you inside a waterfall of rapidly spawning pop-up ads? Why would anyone need to return to such tactics if their offer were truly as great as it sounds? Why do they think that this ploy is OK? The recent record-holder we've seen had eleven (yes, 11) exit stoppers before sanity was restored.

    2) **Incongruence of the inner offer.** OK, it all sounded just too good to pass up, and the entry price was just sooo low that you had to check it out, so you ordered it... and now you're expecting a download, but are confronted with a series of One Time Offers, upsells, down sells, cross sells, etc. This is not an automatic deal breaker -- though annoying, it has become an expected part of the landscape -- **unless** the inner offers contradict the main offer you just bought. For example, something was presented as a turnkey system for $27, but now they want $297/mo. to make it... turnkey. Run. And refund.

There are many more warning signs, but a complete guide is

beyond our scope here. The old saw applies: if an offer seems too good to be true, it might just be a pig with expertly applied lipstick.

So what does all this have to do with rifles and shooting galleries?

Carnival arcades and shooting equipment provide some apt metaphors for illustrating our main point, which is how the application of **executive search techniques,** along with informed **management consulting methods,** can dramatically increase the probability of starting a successful business with a short, careful, fully informed process.

The keys, as in recruiting, are deep knowledge and expert understanding of both sides of the equation: First, **the candidate** (you!), which we'll dive into in a moment; Second, **the opportunity** -- its requirements, costs, difficulties, advantages, drawbacks, profit potentials, benefits, flaws, and competitors.

Both you and the opportunity are entities of great complexity in the equation. Most experienced recruiters will be familiar with the process of discerning your strengths and weaknesses. Only a few will also have the exceptional depth and breadth of experience that comes from consulting in the internet business market -- the complete package required to act as your competent advisor in the selection process. If you are able to work with one, the likelihood of your business succeeding is greatly increased, without the pain and expense of the multiple trial-and-error approach that you face when you have limited experience. (You would surely gain experience along the way, but it would be of the most expensive variety...)

Consider the universe of possible business types, marketing

approaches, and technical skills requirements of the opportunities, and the complexity of finding an optimized solution is crystallized.

Imagine the range and depth of business and product offerings as objects in an arcade shooting gallery -- but each one animated, calling out for your attention, giving you its best pitch, as loudly and as frequently as possible.

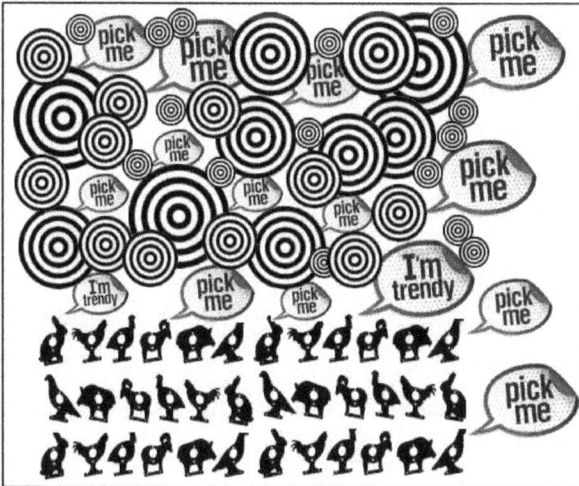

If you have been looking for your ideal opportunity for any length of time, this analogy and illustration will probably resonate.

Each object in it could represent an entire *category* of options, not just a single product or program. Should you look at article writing, niche marketing, blogging, hosting, domain flipping, affiliate marketing? Maybe product retailing, auctions, Amazon, EBay, importing, drop shipping? Perhaps you should write eBooks, or Kindle content, or develop iPad apps, or resell PLR products? Lever a business off of a Facebook presence, or shared interests on Pinterest, or forums, or Twitter? This is only a small sample. The actual list is as limitless as the range of businesses in the brick and mortar world.

Where do you start? *How* **do you start??**

Let's borrow from the approach of experienced headhunters. First, they learn with precision the facets of the position they have been asked to fill. They learn about the industry, usually over a period of years. They learn about the company offering the position; its history, its management, its ethos, its culture. They learn about the hiring process, the committees, the histories of prior presented candidates, the idiosyncrasies of the hiring managers. They learn what characteristics are desirable in an ideal candidate. Only then do they begin looking for candidates that meet or exceed a now very long list of expectations.

The identification of an appropriate candidate begins by compiling a list of objective elements that *must* appear on a person's resume, as well as an additional list of *strongly desired* elements. Databases, networked contacts and various search facilities are used extensively to develop an initial list of possible candidates.

Finally, the recruiter is able to utilize his or her signature skill -- the art of intense conversational listening, aided by an extensive series of expert questions designed to elicit the true strengths and weaknesses of the candidate *vis-a-vis* the focal opportunity. A skilled recruiter starts this interaction with only a few specific questions in mind, but they begin to flow automatically as the threshold qualifiers are met or surpassed.

The recruiter is after much more than a person capable of doing the job at hand. He is paid very well, and diligently seeks **the** *perfect fit*. The candidate who, when put in front of the hiring manager and committees, will form an almost instant mutual bond, because both candidate and company immediately realize that they are a perfect fit *for each other*. When pure excitement flows from both sides out of that initial meeting, the recruiter knows he has done his job well, and that happy customers and truly fulfilled candidates will be the result.

Now let's look at the "candidate" side of the analysis -- you. An accurate self-inventory is crucial to a successful outcome. Returning to our arcade analogy, let's think in terms of the gun and the projectile.

In the carnival midway, the guns provided are little more than oversized metal tubes mounted on wooden stocks, with recycled BB's fed into a compressed air stream when a player pulls the trigger. Because the BB's are well used and thoroughly dented and banged up, and the tube is a loose fit, no two shots will follow the same trajectory. Accuracy is not possible, with the point of impact varying by as much as a foot or so from the aim point.

The shooter will spend his first 10 or 15 shots getting some idea of drop-off and scatter, before trying to track in on a target. We expect this sort of game-rigging in the midway, sloppiness by design that always favors the house. Helps keep the cost of Kewpie dolls down for the operator and all.

If we return to our real world comparison with the internet, few entrepreneurs can afford 10 or 15 sure misses before any possibility of hitting a genuine target. The odds must be narrowed.

So take a gun of your own design to the game. If you think of yourself as the "bullet" in this model, you don't want to be just another banged up recycled BB. You're serious about getting the job done, and you are not interested in being the next sucker. You want to be an armor piercing incendiary tracer!

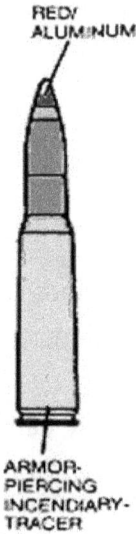

RED/ ALUMINUM

Let's start our self-inventory at the pointy end. Fitting that it is colored red, because it represents your heart. If what you truly LOVE to do can be the leading feature of your business, your chances of success increase dramatically. What do you love? How can it be incorporated into an internet business model?

The next section of the bullet, its core, represents your skill sets: what are your core competencies? What are your computer and internet skills? How much, of what, can you do by yourself?

ARMOR-
PIERCING
INCENDIARY-
TRACER

Inside the casing is the powder, which determines the force of the explosion propelling you to your target. It is the sum of your life experiences, your passions, your enthusiasm, your drive, your resources, and your persistence. You must account for (subtract) your limitations, distractions, and constraints.

Do you have enough net force to propel you through the inevitable obstacles and challenges? Will you persevere and get it done? Can you formulate plans and timelines, and meet your own schedule for deliverables? Do you have the discipline to work when you'd rather relax, with nobody to answer to except yourself? These are fundamental questions that only you can answer, and above all, you must be truthful with yourself.

Moving Forward

We trust that we have triggered some new thought patterns for you here, thoughts that will help you to avoid most of the innumerable pitfalls that await the uninformed masses, seeking to make money online.

We wish you well, and we congratulate you on your decision to join the 1%!

The journey is not easy, but most definitely, **it is worth it!!**

Payday To Playday

About Rick Mortimer

Rick Mortimer has interviewed over 30,000 candidates in his 40+ year business career, and recruited or hired over 2,000 top performers. His experience spans many industries and verticals, with a heavy emphasis on IT and internet, sales and marketing, and finance.

He is a serial entrepreneur, having started his first business at age 16. His startups include the internet service provider *illuma.net* in 1994 (closed 1998), Recruiters' Roundtable Association in 1999, a private online resource for professional recruiters entering its 15th year of continuous service at *r0r.org*, and *recessionconsultants.com* in 2008, which specializes in the internet space. His other businesses have included securities brokerage, trust advisory services, and mortgage finance consulting.

Rick is available to consult with individuals seeking to enter the internet space for generating income through his sites at
InternetMoney.ME,
BootstrapMentor.ME,
BoomerReinvent.ME,
And *GenXReinvent.ME.*

He can also be reached at:

rm@r0r.org (r-zero-r.org)

mortimer@recessionconsultants.com

or through his G+ page: **google.com/+RickMortimer1**

"Search engine marketing and search engine optimization are critically important to online businesses. You can spend every penny you have on a website, but it will all be for nothing if nobody knows your site is there."

~Marc Ostrofsky~

Chapter 11

Partnering and Profiting: Cultivating Powerful and Rewarding Strategic Partnerships Using a Technology Platform

By Sean Wander

Jim's got It all wrong...

Imagine this...you're at an event filled with dozens of bright-eyed, motivated and passionate people around you and all of a sudden a smiling individual, let's call him "Jim," approaches you. With a stack of business cards in hand (or more accurately in the back of his name tag pocket) the first thing he does is pull out his business card and with no real presence, no sign of a real connection yet and let's face it, no real interest in hearing your answer, he asks about you and your business.

At this point you're not even sure you like Jim yet, and the thought of doing business with him hasn't even crossed your mind, but as a polite reflex you take his card and start to answer his question and describe who you are and what you do and as you do a funny thing happens...As you're talking you catch a glimpse of Jim's eyes looking not at you but just over your left shoulder, then quickly and almost imperceptibly to his left and right and then it hits you; you realize that Jim is actually looking around the room for someone "more important" than you that he may need to be speaking with next and because he's not really listening, he doesn't even realize that you, the one right there in his presence, may be the very individual that could add another zero to his bottom line, or even change his life in a very meaningful way.

Having waited for your first pause, Jim now launches into his "presentation" about what he does, which is actually a series of statements and declarations rather than building any real conversation and when he's through, he suggests a follow up conversation where you can discuss joint venturing because clearly, "you've got a lot in common." Then you, like most people, smile and tell him that sounds great and you thank Jim for stopping by, knowing full well this business card will be in very good company with the stack of hundreds, if not thousands of cards you've kept from people you've met at events over the years.

Now it's highly unlikely that even if you have a great memory and a lot of time on your hands you'd actually remember Jim as someone that you need to follow up with, let alone do business with. But what is it specifically about this exchange that misses the mark so badly? It's not inappropriate, really, to suggest that just about everything was wrong, but here's the crux of it.

Jim wasn't connecting on a meaningful level because he wasn't prepared, and he didn't have any real interest in listening so that he *could be prepared* to offer a genuine opportunity for partnership based on the information he absorbed from the conversation. I'm sure you've heard something like this before but it bears repeating...

Good luck (and a good partnership) happens when preparation and opportunity meet.

I'm all for "happy accidents" where two great people find each other and really connect. After all, even our spouses, closest friends and business associates were complete and total strangers at one point. The fact is, had there been any real connection or an effort to make one from either party, even the example with Jim could have turned into something. For me, in order to make the best of those scenarios, I know that I have to prepare myself for the event itself and for potential encounters, and there are a few different ways that I approach this.

Through a combination of conversations with friends and partners, advertised commitments and common sense, I generally have a very good idea who is going to be at a particular event that I'm attending and once I know this, I try to make a list of three to five people that I would really like to connect with there and I focus on them. These are the people that I feel I'm most in alignment with and that potentially, I would have the best chance of adding the greatest value for them in our relationship.

Now I'm not suggesting that it's totally wrong to "work the room" in a more expansive way. I'm simply noting that my preference is to leave every event knowing that I've truly cultivated at least a few really deep and strong connections, rather than exchange dozens of business cards and handshakes (which will always happen anyway); in fact, I don't even use cards myself anymore with all of the other technology available to us.

So once I've selected these individuals, it's now time for me to really dig in and think through how these conversations might shape up in a best case, and also to learn more about them and the nuances of their business if I don't already know the important details. These go beyond their niche and company details; these are the things that really matter to them and sometimes, there is common ground on a passionate subject that has little or nothing to do with their business. The point is that

I'm looking for ways that I can *meaningfully approach and connect* with someone and have a high degree of confidence that the conversation can go well.

I'm considering all of these ideas and notes and incorporating them into what I call my *Relationship Value Proposition* because at some point, the conversation will shift into the mode of "where do we go from here" and the best thing you can ever do for yourself is to...

Remember that it's ALWAYS about THEM...

I can't even begin to tell you how often I come across people who are clearly thinking mostly, if not only, about themselves. All of their energy and focus is spent thinking about how great it would be if they could engage so and so because they'd really help their business so they look to the stages and seek out the "Gurus" and, in the process, they often overlook the incredible pool of talent and resources that are fully engaged in the audience, learning and taking lots of notes.

Having this mindset will make it so much more difficult for someone to find a way to work together with you because what you're focused on is others filling the voids in your business, rather than having total clarity about how you can in fact help others fill the gaps in theirs. Because although it's helpful to know where you need the help when you're asked, it is exponentially more effective to know how you can serve others because you can, in fact, gain everything that you want when all of your intentions and focus are on helping others get what they want.

So, from the prep work that you have done prior to the event, you'll know enough about your target connections to know where you are in alignment and the conversations can begin and develop through these areas. I have seen time and again how powerful it is to cultivate relationships in this manner because inevitably you will learn where this person's challenges are and where there might be an opening. Also, when a relationship kicks off on the right foot, you can always discuss opportunities that may save time, reduce costs or increase revenues dramatically.

Have you ever thought about software?

One of the greatest roles you can step into is that of the person who provides a valuable solution to a key problem, pain or challenge. But many times, these kinds of solutions aren't a novelty; so the next best thing is when you are able to offer some kind of speed and automation for the solution, and one of the most powerful ways you can do this is through the use of software.

When people find a software program that is reliable for them, whether it's used daily or only as needed, they tend to use that program faithfully, and thus they obtain real results. Additionally, our most important technology resources are completely unimpacted by whatever is happening in the world that is meant to create economic fear. Just think about it...when was the last time you refused to open Microsoft Word or your email program because the economy was bad?

A great point of connection occurs on a business level when you can clearly demonstrate for your potential partner how adding software that incorporates their own process or framework for curing their specific customer pain can benefit them, but on top of that, you will offer a complete "dream scenario" when you remember to...

Tee it right up for them...

Despite the fact that you are now bringing something so powerful to someone with a new product offering, you can't ignore the fact that even if they were to make use of this new technology it often creates more objections through successful implementation. With software, for example, having a large volume of sales for that software product may raise the question of who will be handling the technical support for the product, and along with that, who will be responsible for developing the training on using the software part of the solution?

An intelligent and well-prepared strategic partner will have already considered these and many other potential "objections" in advance so that any time these challenges arise, there is a simple and mutually beneficial solution for them. Simply put, when you're preparing for and engaging this process, you are looking to take away any possible reason for someone to say no to you because you are certain that when the peanut butter meets the chocolate in your future relationship, the results will be magnificent.

A case study worth noting...

Perhaps the best way to put this all together is to share a little about how one of my greatest partnerships with Mike Filsaime and Andy Jenkins and their Marketing Genesis brand came to pass.

When you're fortunate enough to be in a mastermind group or think tank of some kind, you are already in a great position because not only are you often gaining access to cutting edge best practices, you are also placing yourself in a perfect position to serve others. My relationship with Mike really developed through his own mastermind where we shared many occasions to help people in the process of their own business review and improvement.

Over time, he came to learn more and more about what my partner Mitchell and I do and naturally, I was already quite familiar with his business, but as our friendship grew, so did the level of intimacy as it pertained to some of our greatest successes and lessons learned. When we sat together at an event in FL over the summer, we had just come out with our latest software product called Presentation Control, which provides a powerful and profitable framework for delivering presentations on stage or online. Mike was very intrigued by this and we started to think about how we might be able to form a version of the software that incorporates the best of our Control Writer technology with a powerful marketing framework for creating offers and campaigns around them.

And so along with other very interesting discoveries, like the fact that Andy Jenkins and my partner Mitchell had been roommates for two and a half years while at NYU, we stayed the course, getting together and really hashing out the framework and using software as a way to add speed and automation to the solution. But I assure you...absolutely none of this would have happened had I walked up to Mike or Andy at an event or even on the Marketer's Cruise and said:

"Mike, I know you're really busy but at some point on this cruise, if I could just get five minutes of your time to talk about possibly joint venturing with you, I'm sure it would really be great."

Next action steps...

If anything I've shared with you in this chapter has made sense to you, let's be sure that you really get the most benefit and put these thoughts into action. So here are three things you can do to get a huge jumpstart on your next potential strategic partnership:

1. Make a list of the next 2-3 events that you are most likely to attend and write down specifically why you feel that you must attend them.
2. Identify at least 3 people for each event that you know you'd like to connect with, and get very clear on exactly where you feel that you can provide the most value for THEM and not the other way around.
3. Do your research and be prepared with conversations and positioning that will allow you to present a dream partnership scenario that few are likely to refuse. In other words, make it nearly impossible for them to say no.

I believe that every real connection and every chance meeting brings with it the power and the promise to create something incredible...something the world has never seen before, and a friendship that could last a lifetime.

My greatest wish is that you remember this every time you meet someone, or hope to meet someone, and you recognize and cherish the incredible opportunities and individuals that you encounter with every passing moment.

Payday To Playday

About Sean Wander

Sean is a contributing author in the book *The Power of a Mastermind,* which he co-wrote with dozens of leaders in the marketing and personal growth industries, and his first solo book: *Soul Matrix: Embrace Life's Drama and Discover Your True Inner Voice* is slated for release in February of 2014. He is an international speaker of more than 11 years, speaking on various topics based on his expertise in the film industry, strategic marketing, software technology and personal development.

He is the Co-Founder and CEO of Control Influence LLC, an umbrella company for Reelwriting, LLC, where he and his partners Mitchell German and Howard Reichman align with industry talent and aspiring talent to develop projects for the film and television world, and Control Writer Software which provides productivity and creative project based software for multiple industries.

Among them are the software titles: "Plot Control" for film, "Sales Message Control" for Sales and Marketing and "Presentation Control" for delivering powerful and profitable presentations online or onstage. For his latest project he has partnered with Internet giants Mike Filsaime and Andy Jenkins for "Offer Control" software and their upcoming launch of Offer Genesis.

Sean's greatest passion lies in speaking to groups and individuals, helping them through spiritual, creative and strategic blocks so they can make the connections and decisions that will yield the greatest results in their lives.

He has been an advisor or an officer for numerous seven and eight figure businesses at various stages of company growth in various disciplines including strategic marketing, personal development, finance and even manufacturing for the architectural and design marketplace. While at Oppenheimer in the financial sector, he was part of a team with more than $250 Million in assets under management.

Sean holds a B.A. from Arizona State University and supports a number of charitable causes. Born and raised in New York, he now lives with his wife and two sons in Palm Beach, FL.

Websites:

controlwriter.com

reelwriting.com

seanwander.com

Chapter 12

How Many Times Have You Heard It:
STORIES SELL!
By Mitchell German

For anyone who comes in contact with the marketing world, among the first things they'll hear is that they need to use stories in their marketing. Every marketing "Guru" talks about the importance of a good story, every training course advocates developing a story, and every major launch is rooted in a great story.

If you're like me, you've heard about all the different types of stories: "Home town boy makes good" … "The Accidental Discovery" … "The Reluctant Hero" … "Us against them" … And the list goes on.

But here's the problem: It's easy for all the gurus to talk about stories and say you need to have a good story, but what exactly is a "good story?" What is the "right story?" How do you find your story, and how in the world do you integrate that story with rest of your marketing?

At this point, let me take bit of a detour, and tell you a little bit about myself… a story, if you will. I went to NYU Film School and graduated in 1993 (which also happens to be the same class as the "Boss" man himself, Andy Jenkins).

From there I worked in the film business and did most of my work as a screenwriter or more specifically, a script doctor; essentially I'd fix other people's screenplays. On the whole I was probably just an average screenwriter, until I saw the movie "Liar Liar."

"Liar Liar" is the movie with Jim Carrey in which he plays an attorney who can't tell a lie. I became obsessed with this movie and reverse engineered it to better understand how the writers got the different layers to work so seamlessly together.

Now I've done a specific test many times and the results are always the same... What I do is ask people what the movie "Liar Liar" is about. Take a second right now and think about it; what *is* the movie "Liar Liar" about? For the most part I usually get an answer similar to how I just framed it: "It's about an attorney who can't tell a lie" or "It's about a boy who makes a wish that his father can't tell a lie." And those answers are true, but for one tiny little itty-bitty problem... THAT'S NOT WHAT THAT MOVIE IS ABOUT!

What then is "Liar Liar" about? It's about an attorney who must win a specific legal case and to do so he must be able to lie about the facts... and that's why his son's wish that he cannot tell a lie is SO significant! The inability to lie only becomes truly significant in the context of the legal case, and the legal case only becomes interesting because he can't lie.

Understanding this is key; the movie is about all the related storylines, all at the same time. It's NOT just a story about a boy and his father. It's NOT just a story about a boy who makes a wish. It's NOT just a story about an attorney who can't tell a lie. And it's NOT just a story about some attorney who needs to win some legal case. The magic of the story happens when all of these parts are combined.

It's the combination and seamless integration of the different layers and individual storylines that make "Liar Liar" a great movie. And "Liar Liar" is NOT unique. All the great movies have the same layering of related and relevant multiple storylines going on.

So "Liar Liar" was the movie that truly opened my eyes to what was really going on in the great movies. Ultimately I went on to identify what I call the "8 Core Elements" of a great movie, and from these Core Elements I created a 12-part Structured Timeline. All totaled, these 20 parts of a movie are the distilled essence of what makes a film great, and over the years I've broken down upwards of 100 of the most successful movies to demonstrate this.

Based on this information I created a screenwriting training course and a piece of software called Plot Control. From there I started to learn about marketing myself so I could sell my course and software.

It was at that point I kept coming across the notion that you need a really good story as part of your marketing, but I didn't have one. Think about that... there I was, the screenwriting script doctor who had built a course on how to write movies and create great stories and I was completely stymied about what story to use for my marketing.

Now I consider myself to be somewhat clever, so I thought I'd use my software, which is meant for creating movies, to create my marketing story. A few days later, although I had the makings of a bad movie about my life, I had nothing that resembled a marketing story. It was then I realized that stories for movies were far too complex for marketing, while the really good marketing stories were simple yet poignant, relevant and complex all at the same time.

So I decided to try and figure out what is going on with these marketing stories, beyond the simple genre or type. I decided I was going to break down fundamentally how they were built. And what I found was that there were SEVEN specific parts that are common in almost all of the stories I came across.

So I mapped them out, and developed what I call the **Story Foundation Blueprint**:

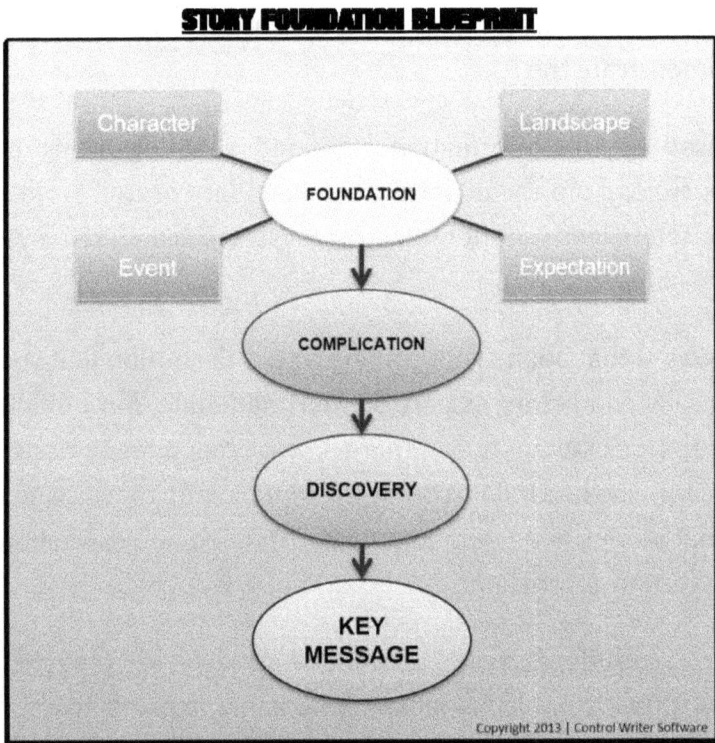

STORY FOUNDATION BLUEPRINT

Character

Landscape

FOUNDATION

Event

Expectation

COMPLICATION

DISCOVERY

KEY MESSAGE

Copyright 2013 | Control Writer Software

This simple visual breakdown shows the seven key parts that are required for a "story" to actually be a "story."

Let me quickly walk you through it.

The **Foundation Layer** is comprised of four of the seven parts: *Character, Landscape, Event and Expectation.* If you look at the diagram you'll notice that each one is linked to the Foundation.

These four parts establish the framework upon which the rest of the story is built. (It's important to note that the foundation alone is NOT enough, and many make the mistake of creating a story foundation as their "story," but they go no further.)

The Foundation of the story needs to do a few things. Most obvious is that it must establish the key parts of the story already mentioned, but more than that it must anchor the story to the product or service being offered. For a story to be most effective there must always be a relationship that links the story to the product or service, and the clearer and more direct that relationship, the more powerful and effective the story will ultimately be. The Foundation must also lay the framework for the story type, such as "Accidental Discovery" or "Reluctant Hero," etc.

Let's take a look at the four parts of the Foundation:

1. **Character:** This is simply who the story is about. In marketing stories, people are typically telling their own story, so they are in essence the main character. So in your stories, it will be you.
2. **Landscape:** These are the parameters in which the story takes place, such as location and time, and other details.
3. **Event:** This is what is specifically taking place in the life of the main character. A good story is not based on a typical day… it should be based on an "*exceptional*" day. (It's worth noting that an "event" is part of the Foundation, but most people make the mistake of making the "event" their whole story.)

4. **Expectation:** This is the "Anticipated Outcome" of the character of the story based on the Event that is taking place.

So here's where we're at in terms of our Foundation:

*There is a **Character** in some **Landscape** that has an **Event** taking place in their life and because of this they have an **Expectation** for a certain outcome.*

All of these of course must be related to/and anchor the product or service in some way, but a good story does not end here.

You see as the story progresses, it moves towards the fulfillment of the character's expectation, but then they will encounter some type of **Complication**.

You'll notice that the complication is next on the diagram, and this is simply an unforeseen turn of events that makes it unlikely that the character's expectation will be met in the way he or she expected.

But this is *still* not enough.

The story continues and because of this complication the character must now make a **Discovery**. This could be simple or complex, but the discovery itself must be a direct outcome of the complication; in other words it is ONLY because of the complication that the character makes this discovery.

A fantastic example of this occurred in the corporate world with 3M. When they invented Post-Its they were actually trying to make a better super glue, but they ran into a Complication because the glue never set completely and instead remained sticky. What happened next? They <u>Discovered</u> that the "bad" glue could be reused, which in turn led to Post-Its.

Notice that they didn't want to invent Post-Its, nor were they interested in glue that was reusable. I imagine the initial reaction to the glue not setting was considered a significant failure. Yet without that failure, they would never have made the discovery that led to Post-Its.

Finally, you need a **KEY MESSAGE**. The story has to have a point, and ideally that point needs to be about your product or story... this is your Key Message.

So with my new marketing story framework in hand, here's what my story became...

> Character = Me
> Landscape = Film business
> Event = Doing basic screenwriting work
> Expectation = I'd been an average screenwriter
> Complication = Saw Liar Liar and became obsessed with understanding it better
> Discovery = Identified the 8 Core Elements
> Key Message = Use these 8 Core Elements if you want to write a screenplay that will truly work as a movie.

If you thumb back a page or two, you'll see this is the EXACT story I told you in explaining who I am. It's my story, or at least the one I use when I am selling my screenwriting software Plot Control.

The cool part about the Story Foundation Blueprint is that you can use it for every story, from the most simple to those that are more complex. And you can use it for a story within a story. And it always works when used correctly.

Take this story, for example:

My partner in the software business is Sean Wander. Sean is the guy in the business that does all the elbow rubbing and event participation. So he was at Mike Filsaime's mastermind in early 2013 and ended up sitting right next to Mike at one of the dinners. He took the opportunity to tell Mike about our Control Writer software, which at that point we were developing for use beyond just the screenwriting marketplace. Mike was really interested in the software and the possibility of helping to promote it or maybe even making a version together with him. They left the mastermind with the intent to follow up once the software was a little more developed and ready for deployment in other markets.

So stepping away from this story for just one second, you'll notice I did a few things...
Character = Sean
Landscape = Mike Filsaime mastermind
Event = Ends up sitting next to Mike at dinner and shows him the software
Expectation = They intend to hook up and work together on the software.
Now back to the story...

As you can imagine, Sean and myself were pretty stoked about this opportunity; after all, Mike had enormous reach and influence in the Internet Marketing world. Unfortunately that reach and influence was a little too good because Mike ended up on a beach in Turks and Caicos with Andy Jenkins. It was there that they decided to join together and do the Video Genesis launch.

So the next time Sean met up with Mike, well, he got some bad news. It turned out that Mike was going to be focusing all of his efforts, at least in the near term, on growing his business with Andy.

You can imagine Sean was disappointed, so he turned aside and texted me an update... the text said something like: *"Things not looking good... Mike F is working Andy Jenkins now and it could be a while before he can work with us."*

Now here's the interesting thing... remember I mentioned a little earlier that I was in the same graduating class as Andy Jenkins at NYU Film School? Well that wasn't the whole story... I was actually _roommates and close friends_ with Andy for years.

So I texted back to Sean... "This is awesome news. I was roommates with Andy Jenkins when I went to NYU!"

Now I wasn't there, but Sean tells the story that he read the message and wasn't really sure what to make of it, so he said to Mike... "Did you know that my partner Mitch was roommates with Andy at NYU?"

Mike had no idea if that was true or not, so he texted Andy... "Do you know a guy name Mitch German?"

To which Andy responded something like... **"I was roommates with a Mitch German at NYU for a 2 ½ years. Why do you ask?"**

Now let's break away from the story for a moment and look at what just happened...
> Complication: Mike is now partnering with Andy, so he can't do the software.
> Discovery: Mitch was roommates and old buddies of the

Boss man himself!

Finally we need to end this story with a Key Message, and that Key Message needs to be related to the product or service that we are promoting, which when we use this story, would be the software Offer Control that we have now created together with Mike and Andy.

So for us, one possible Key Message is about the creation of the software itself: *The joining together of the power of our Control Writer software with the marketing minds of Mike Filsaime and Andy Jenkins.*

Or we could use a more metaphysical Key Message, such as: *The universe conspired to make sure the world had this software Offer Control, which combines the power of our Control Writer software and the marketing genius of Mike Filsaime and Andy Jenkins.*

I hope this information and the Story Foundation Blueprint helps you to focus in on and create your own story that you can use in your marketing and sales campaigns.

If you are interested in getting more information from us about the Story Foundation Blueprint or Offer Control software, please drop a quick note to myself, Sean or both of us at **support@controlwriter.com.**

Payday To Playday

About Mitchell German

Mitchell German is the creator of Control Writer Software and its unique approach which provides a user with maximum creativity while working within a highly structured framework. Mitchell attended NYU Tisch School of the Arts and graduated in 1993. He has worked as a filmmaker, screenwriter, script doctor, and screenplay consultant for 17 years. Mitchell created the first instance of Control Writer Software as Plot Control based on his screenwriting techniques known as the Thematic Gap and the Core Elements. He has since partnered with Sean Wander to expand and build the Control Writer brand, with current iterations including Plot Control, Presentation Control, Sales Message Control, and Offer Control. (Offer Control was also developed together with Mike Filsaime and Andy Jenkins.)

"*Never trust anyone who has not brought a book with them.*"

~Lemony Snicket~

Chapter 13

If You're Stuck In A Rut, You'll Always Be There Unless You Take Massive Action

By David Cavanagh

Like all good stories, this one starts off with "Once Upon A Time"...

Once upon a time, there was a guy named David Cavanagh who was totally broke (no money), was a single father of a beautiful daughter named Krystal and was told by everyone how smart and awesome he was, yet he could barely pay his rent each week.

Too bad for being so "smart and awesome!" Can you relate to this in any way, shape or form?

David had to be the life of every party he attended; he was the "comedian and joker" everyone had to have around, but the "inside" of David was definitely not what he was portraying on the "outside."

You see, David was a very lonely man who was crying out to be loved, to be wanted, to be noticed, to be listened to and he did everything just to be the centre of attention.

Basically, this attention fed David's ego and low self-esteem to the point where it put a smile on his face. It kept him feeling "okay to be alive," so to speak.

David was living in Mudgeeraba on the Gold Coast in Queensland, Australia and his only form of income was collecting a single parent's pension each fortnight to help him and his daughter survive.

He was sharing a 3 bedroom townhouse with a guy named Dennis Hall, and he could barely pay Dennis the half rent he owed each week. Life was definitely not pleasant for David Cavanagh - in fact, it was living hell at the time.

Then one day while David was at home lying on his couch, he got a phone call. The phone call was from Adam Hudson who was running a company called the "Better Business Institute."

This company was actually run by Peter Sun and Adam Hudson; two very talented marketers and entrepreneurs who had kicked several home runs in many of their previous businesses.

Picture this - David was sitting at home and got this phone call at 7:52pm in the evening.

The conversation on the phone went something like this:

"Hi David, it's Adam. Peter Sun and I are looking for someone to help with our in-house Internet Marketing, and when we sat down and brainstormed, the name that kept coming into our heads was David Cavanagh. Do you mind coming in for an interview with Pete and I tomorrow morning?"

Of course David said "yes" and the following day David went in to see Adam and Peter.

Now I'll recall everything as it happened, but looking back at it from January 2014:

When I was being interviewed back then, Adam told me how I was a really talented guy. He said I was an immensely talented guy when it came to copywriting, sales, motivation, personal development, persuasion, internet, seo, etc. I felt so good when Adam complimented me because it filled my low self-esteem bucket and made me feel wanted, noticed, accepted and loved.

It was like "Wow, I can't believe I'm hearing all these great comments about me."

Then Adam dropped the bombshell on the conversation:

"The only thing is, David, you're focusing your energy 1% on 100 things, rather than putting 100% energy and focus onto 1 thing. If Peter and I are to employ you, you really need to stop these habits and do everything the way we tell you, or you won't have a job."

That was the part of the conversation that pissed me off big time!

You see, I didn't know whether to take his comment as a huge insult, or to shut up and put my pride and ego to the side and simply keep listening to him.

After all, he had invited me in for an interview, so he must have felt I was worth talking to in the first place, don't you think?

Have you ever had the feeling of being down in the dumps, not knowing what to do with your life?

The feeling of not knowing who to turn to for help? The lack of thoughts of not knowing what direction you should be taking? And yet, I was so good at telling others what to do!

This was me back then. This was a totally different David Cavanagh to the David Cavanagh of 2014 and beyond.

But I could have stayed the same. I could have kept talking

rubbish to myself. I could have kept going on and on with the never ending thoughts of how good I was, how I was better than everyone else, how I knew everything about anything... even though I was struggling to pay my bills, struggling to put food in my mouth each week and the ongoing hassles of keeping the debt collectors away from my front door.

I really needed to change everything in my life, and Adam's words were the catalyst for me to start changing immediately.

Three months after working with Adam and Peter I was told by the guys in the office how they were all flying down from the Gold Coast to Sydney to see Tony Robbins at a seminar called "Unleash the Power Within." I knew I had to be at this event. Something inside of me said "Do whatever it takes to get to this event, David."

I asked Peter and Adam if they could pay for me, and I promised I'd pay them back each week out of my salary. It was putting myself into another "financial hassle," but my gut feeling told me that I just had to do it.

I flew down to the Tony Robbins seminar and made some totally crazy commitments to myself while I was there. I even wrote them into the book I was given and when I got back to the Gold Coast I read them out to myself.

"Get out of the relationship you're currently in…. buy a brand new car…. stop focusing on helping everyone else and start looking after yourself for once in your life…. leave Peter and Adam and work on stages all around the World teaching people how to make money on the Internet."

Once I re-read everything I wrote, I thought I must have been delusional. I wondered how in the World I would ever accomplish one of these far-fetched goals (let alone accomplish them all).

Well, I took massive action and made sure I put my heart and soul into achieving my goals and outcomes that I wrote in my book at the seminar. I knew I needed to do whatever it took at the time (and beyond) to become the David I knew I could become.

Was it hard? Yes, it was extremely difficult! There were numerous times I felt like giving up, but giving up was what I'd always done, so that wasn't an option for me anymore. I'd given up, failed and quit too many times in the past, so it was time for change.

Am I glad I took massive action to achieve my goals and come out bigger and better on the other side? You better believe it! I'm extremely happy, as it's my made life much better in so many ways. Ways in which I could never write about on paper.

Today I travel the World teaching people how to make money online. I've spoken at nearly all of the biggest Internet seminars, workshops and events in the World. I've been voted Best Speaker at a lot of the seminars I've spoken at (which I'm very proud of).

I also run 8, 10 and 12 day internet marketing workshops in Pattaya Beach, Thailand with Roger Bourdon, Eric Zeitoun and Nisarat Pongroka (my coaching team) with students flying in from all over the World to attend. Who would have thought back then that David Cavanagh would change so much and be able to achieve all of this?

In closing, my tips for you for 2014 and beyond are:

You can achieve anything you want, if you firstly make a decision to do whatever it takes to achieve them.

Secondly, you mustn't listen to the people who bring you down. You mustn't listen to your family who tell you it can't be done.

Thirdly, you must take massive action and do everything within your power to achieve your goals, dreams and outcomes.

Fourthly, never ever give up. If you need extra help, ask someone. If you need a push, join a mastermind. Contact me for advice.

You must listen to the "inner you" that realizes anything can be done if you make a decision and act upon it!

Information without implementation is just "more information." Implement whatever you know needs to be done, and at the end of the day just remember that the only truth is the end result. It's no good talking about what you're going to do - go out there and do it.

Go out and get the results you truly deserve! Make yourself, your family and your friends proud of the "new you," and may 2014 be your best year ever!

Payday To Playday

About David Cavanagh

David Cavanagh has over 30 years' experience in sales, marketing and coaching and has sold millions of dollars of products and services in over 13 countries.

He's a leading authority on how to get started on the internet, whether you're a beginner, an intermediate or highly skilled and need to take your business to the next level.

David was born in Australia to parents with very little money, yet took his income from $250 a week in 2003 to over $1,000,000 a year in less than 3 years with his simple step by step A to Z online system.

He has won numerous "Best Speaker" awards at seminars all around the World, as well as hundreds of sales and marketing accolades and testimonials from his students and industry professionals.

A former DJ, David increased his income from $7,800 to $247,000 in 51 days when he managed to secure 32 clubs to employ him and his team of disc jockeys when he started the Disc Jockey Booking Centre in Sydney, Australia.

He loves to have fun and enjoys an incredible lifestyle in Pattaya Beach, Thailand.

He has a heart of gold and is known for massively over-delivering because of his passion for helping people succeed and make money online and offline.

He's spoken on stages with well-known professionals such as Jim Rohn, Jay Abraham, Robert Allen, Mike Filsaime, Tom Beal, Armand Morin, Pat Mesiti, Nik Halik, Mal Emery, Fabian Lim, Jeff and Kane, Joel Bauer, Brett McFall, Tom Hua and many more.

David now has coaches he employs in Australia, UK, Dubai, USA, Singapore and in Thailand to help, support, assist and nurture over 7,000 students.

He believes "the only truth is the end result" and wants you to experience exceptional results for your business from the moment you start working with him.

If you truly want to become an industry leader, want to make more money on the internet than you've ever imagined, start a business (or taking your online or offline business to the next level) and do what you want, when you want and become an industry rockstar, then David Cavanagh is the man you need to get to know immediately.

So if you're prepared to do whatever it takes to move forward in life, then contact David at **david@davidcavanagh.com** for any help and assistance, or visit his website at **www.davidcavanagh.com**

Chapter 14

Offline Strategies To Make Massive Online Income
By Gus Sevilla

One of the questions I get asked frequently is "can someone really make money online?"

My answer is always YES.

Unfortunately, many people think that "internet marketing" equals "instant riches," and that is far from reality. My advice is to set attainable goals. For example, do not expect to make a million dollars over the weekend, but instead set a goal of maybe an extra $100 a month, or perhaps an extra $10 a day. Or maybe replace your salary so you can leave your day job. Get my drift?

But how can you make money?

Reaching out to your desired market can be very challenging. We, as marketers, have been forced to be more creative with our strategies and turn our marketing more into "interruption" marketing. After all, with so many distractions like social media sites, text messages and cell phones going off all the time, and 3,000 television channels at your fingertips, it's hard to get your market's attention.

Not only that, but with so many changes in Google, it's hard to keep up with all their updates, and many times all our efforts creating blogs, building links, writing articles, optimizing keywords, go down the drain in a matter of seconds.

And this is why many people fail.

Because of these and many other reasons, many people easily give up their dreams and their chances in attaining a successful online business and claiming a piece of the pie of billions of dollars spent on the net every year, and this is because they quit too early.

The secret is to keep focused, keep learning, but most importantly, apply what you have learned.

I've been involved in many affiliate networks, including CPA networks, and use different types of traffic like PPC, CPV, media buys, solo ads, and many more.

Lately I have been testing different offline strategies to make online income.

One of those strategies is using flyers.

I've been using flyers to promote different digital products from networks like ClickBank, and including different CPA offers. It's pretty cheap to print. You can even use your own printer, or if you want to step it up a notch, you can send it to a professional printer and get them done postcard size.

There are different strategies you can use to promote your products using flyers, and I'm going to share 3 that have worked very well for me.

The first thing you need to do is to buy a domain name related to the offer you're promoting. You can then design a flyer using Fiverr for only $5 (Amazing!). Put a catchy headline, a call to action, and make sure you place the domain name in big towards the bottom.

You will then redirect the domain name to your affiliate link. You can easily do this thru your domain registrar, or with a simple PHP script.

Afterwards, you need to print your flyers on regular letter size paper (8.5" x 11"). You will put 4 flyers in one sheet. Then you make 100 copies at Staples for about 5 cents a copy. A total of 5 bucks.

Cut the paper in 4, you now have 400 flyers. Pretty easy huh?

Start putting them in laundromats, on car windshields, on poles, etc. Pretty soon you will start making sales and finding yourself printing more flyers.

The second strategy is instead of redirecting the domain name to just ONE offer, you rotate the link to 3 different offers and see which one converts better.

This can easily be done with a PHP script, and once the visitor types your domain, it goes to 3 different offers, one at a time. This way you can see which product makes you more money, and then once you find the winner, you can easily change the redirect link to just that one offer because you know it will convert.

The third strategy is very simple.

As you probably already know, the money is in the list. What you will do with this strategy is instead of redirecting your domain directly to the offer, you will send the visitor to a landing page and give them a free report of something related to the product you are trying to promote.

Once you have their name and email, you can easily send them more offers using your auto responder. This way you can make more money with different offers in the future.

These 3 strategies using flyers have done wonders for my business. It's easy to implement, and very inexpensive to start.

The best part is that you don't have competition. Not many affiliates are doing this, therefore, you will be the only one doing it.

This is just a few of the strategies I use. The main thing is to stay creative, and most importantly NEVER give up.

If you want more information you can visit my blog: www.AfiliadoSecreto.com.

WARNING: it's in Spanish...hahaha, but it's ok, you can always contact me in English.

Best of luck, and never, EVER give up!

About Gus Sevilla

Gus Sevilla is a business entrepreneur and full time internet marketer for over a decade.

Gus has promoted countless digital and physical products from different affiliate networks and is involved in multiple CPA networks. He uses innovative and creative strategies, perhaps a bit controversial, to attract and convert traffic into sales.

As an expert, Gus has participated in several seminars, either as an attendee or as a speaker, and is a member of many intensive mastermind groups with renowned marketers of this community.

All this has been done in the English market since Gus was born, raised, and live in New York City. However, in late 2010, he entered the Hispanic market with unparalleled success. In fact, in late 2011 he released his first info-product, "Afiliados Delta" (Delta Affiliate).

The launch was a total success, and made over $200,000 in less than 5 days.

The product was one of the most successful in this niche in the Latin market, including ClickBank, one of the largest networks of digital products, which recognized it as one of the best releases and congratulated him on such a great success.

Gus's blog, www.AfiliadoSecreto.com (Secret Affiliate) is one of the most visited in the Latin market for the making money niche, and he has added thousands of subscribers to his list in a very short time.

Chapter 15

Taking It To The Next Level With
The Movers and Shakers
By John Cornetta

Like the majority of internet marketers, I didn't start my business career working online. I was an off-line kind of guy. But I was a self-starter. In 1991 I moved to Atlanta, Ga. with $700 in my pocket. By 2008, I was doing over $7 million in business. I owned a chain of retail stores in Atlanta, published several trade publications, ran industry conventions, nightclubs, restaurants, and employed over 300 people. In 2010, not only was I going through an ugly divorce, but the economy bottomed out. I ended up having a fire sale on most of my businesses, selling them for pennies on the dollar.

When my businesses were doing well, I was living the good life on a $30K monthly salary and I really wanted to be able to keep that lifestyle. I started looking into network marketing, and I noticed that a friend of mine was getting 50-60 new leads a day, where I was only getting 2 or 3 leads, so I asked him what his secret was. He said "squeeze pages." "What are those?" I asked. Needless to say, he taught me about squeeze pages.

For the next 4-5 months I literally spent 18 hours a day at my computer just clicking every link I could click, signing up for every single list I could sign up for, reading emails, just totally submerging myself, gaining new knowledge. Unfortunately, it was not the only thing I gained. Eating breakfast, lunch at dinner at my computer packed on 100 lbs the first 2 years!

Through this all I had some income coming in from the businesses

I sold, my father had passed away, and I moved back to South Florida. It was a tough time.

But all in all, when I had my businesses, and when I was acting in theaters and on the big screen, I was lucky enough that I had a little knack - a knack to identify who the movers and the shakers are and getting to know them very quickly by helping them out in any way I can. I would provide my services to them; I would look at something they might be doing wrong, and given my skill set would help them out, without asking for anything in return. Very quickly, within the first 8 months of moving back to Florida, I got to know a lot of people in the Internet Marketing world; not just knowing them in name only, but actually trading phone numbers, Skyping with them, and generally helping them in their businesses.

These were the movers and shakers like Matt Bacak, Tom Beal, Devon Brown, Brad Fallon, Mike Lewis, Mike Filsaime, and Rich Schefren, just to name a few. I came on their radar really, really quick.

Mike Filsaime and I would talk back and forth and he became a client, buying traffic from me. I was the first person he bought solo ads from. That was a big deal. After my first Marketers Cruise 3 years ago, Mike was kind enough to invite me to his private chat group for him and his employees, helping with each other's launches. I was lucky enough to take the skill I was best at — finding out who's the top people in the market, who they want to emulate, what they need help with, helping them, being genuine, and being really good at what I did - paid traffic, solo ads, Facebook ads, and maximizing clicks.

Now what really blew me up on the scene was that I was getting huge results, and I hate to say this, but I didn't even know the kind of results I was generating! So a gentleman by the name of David Eisner was interviewing me for a short blog, and it turned into a 90 minute interview, which turned into a WSO.

Now, I never even received a dollar from this, or seen the list, but rumor has it that it is the #1 selling interview in the history of the Warrior Forum. It's had over 55,000 page views of the thread, and over 15,000 copies of the interview have been sold. This put me on the top of everyone's radar. But I thought, oh no, I gave away too much information, I gave away the farm. But then I realized that I had a lot more to give, that I didn't give it all away.

Doing that one thing really took me to the next level.

Being Validated

At one point I joined a mastermind, (which *everyone* needs to do) and I was getting attacked for things I was posting. I was told I shouldn't do this and I shouldn't do that, and I couldn't believe it because I knew I was right in what I was saying. But then I was pm'd by Matt Bacak, who told me that I was so far beyond these people, that they don't know what they are talking about, don't listen to them, and that I was on the right track. WOW! To get validated by Matt Bacak was a big thing for me. I knew his reputation, and even though we had both lived in Atlanta, we had never met. But because of the interaction with him on the mastermind we went on to do several projects together, including "41 Tricks to Increase Your Clicks." He was recently working on a giveaway event for one of his clients, so I spent an hour or so with Matt and his support guy going over different ways to set up the script, set up the event, promote the event, etc. I expected nothing in return, but Matt posted a big thanks on

Facebook saying how I'm such a nice guy and how I helped rock it for him.

On one of the Marketers Cruises I met Willy Crawford. We sat down and talked in length about some of the things that could better help him in his business. After the cruise he emailed me a message saying "check this out." It was a video testimonial from Willy. I don't see many of those out there to marketers from Willy Crawford.

Another time Dr. Benny Morris was in one of my Skype channels. We kept getting virus-infected spam messages from him, so I had no choice but to block him. He came back in under another identity and told me that he had been hacked, apologized profusely for the problems that were caused, and asked to come back in to the group. I called him on Skype and told him that if he trusted me to let me take over his computer remotely, while he watched, I could take care of this mess that was created for him. For over 2 hours I cleaned up his computer, defragged it, loaded another anti-virus program, etc. I did this expecting nothing in return. His gift to me was a message with a video testimonial that is just incredible.

Another great person I got to work with was Rick Schefren. I sold traffic to him. Unfortunately he only made 1 or two sales, and after trying to figure out what the problem was, I told him that his conversion rate was set too high. I told him that I would give him 500 subscribers on the house, but that we had to do things my way. Well, he made four sales on a $3,000 product immediately. He ended up making his money back, with a profit, and repaid me with coaching for free, whenever I needed it. Getting perks by helping marketers is priceless. I could never pay for the things that I've gotten from top marketers.

Multiple Skype Groups

One day a marketer friend from Australia, Andrew Looney, had asked me how many Skype groups I had. My reply was "what is a Skype group?" I didn't even know that multiple Skype groups even existed. So he put me in two groups. In one of the groups the guy was a totalitarian...rules on top of rules on top of rules. Now I was a staunch defender of the 1st amendment. I was in court and fighting and winning 1st Amendment cases, and I couldn't tolerate this. So I created my own room, without rules. Well, just one rule - no hate speeches. Eventually my one room turned into ten rooms, with 300 people in each room. And each room was a different niche- solo ads, swaps, discussions, coaching, etc.

Not only did it allow me to sell inside the rooms, but it allowed me to have instant access with 100% deliverability, along with the ability to drive a lot of JV's to product launches. Plus, since I had a huge list, I was able to reciprocate with others in the rooms. But I never go in saying "give me, give me, give me." I go in saying "here, this is what I have to offer you."

I've also been able to duplicate this process with several Facebook groups as well. And I'm starting to lean more towards Facebook because they now have free video calls just like Skype, and as soon as Facebook comes up with sharing the screen feature, I think Skype is going to be pretty well done.

For me, Internet Marketing is a broad term and I like to stay ahead of the curve. Besides selling solo ads and my core business of selling lots of traffic to a lot of big marketers I also have several high end coaching programs, with 10 projects coming online in 2014, plus my own book, collaborating with Mike Lewis, working

141

with Tom Beal on "Fly on The Wall," Frank Salinas, Ali Chowdhry, Jon Tarr and many others. 2014 will be the year of collaborating. I like to bring in other marketers to see what they are doing, and see how we can work together.

The bottom line is if you are looking for quality traffic, looking to increase your conversions, building your lists faster, learning the business, building a solo ad business, marketing your business, and working with a top-notch coach that really cares, I'm here and I'm available.

About John Cornetta

Having moved quickly up the Internet Marketing ladder, John Cornetta is now one of the top authorities on Solo Ads and Paid Traffic. Today John Masterminds with the "Who's Who" of Internet Marketing and runs several high end coaching programs.

To learn more about John, visit him at **www.johncornetta.com**.

"If your actions inspire others to dream more, learn more, do more and become more, you are a leader."

~John Quincy Adams ~

Chapter 16

Evidence of The Published Word
by Carolyn Lewis

For thousands of years authors have been regarded with respect and admiration. And since they wrote the book, one word always came to mind....expert.

Authors tend to find themselves in the crowd that is the "cream of the crop." Being an author is the definitive demarcation line of attack, as it truly separates you from the pack. Whether you decide to write your own book, use a ghostwriter, or be included in a Multi Author book with other leaders, there's no better way for you to create yourself as an authority. Once your potential customers realize that you are a published expert, they will be ready to work with you, as well as refer others.

Most authors do not write their books for the money. Believe it or not, there really is very little money in books, unless you are a J.K.Rowling, or Donald Trump. In the real world of book writing, the actual purpose isn't the book. It's all about what the book **will do for you**. It's all about the new opportunities that will be created, as well as all the doors that will finally open for you.

Let's explore some of the concrete benefits that becoming a published author will afford you:

- New-found respect and admiration
- Personal satisfaction
- Enhanced credibility
- Expert status with your customers
- New customer surge due to your increased credibility

- Businesses, opportunities, and people will naturally seek you out
- High sense of accomplishment
- Newfound connections and increased earnings

Being an author can double, triple, or even quadruple your chances of getting every customer you meet as a client. You'll profit from being an author for your entire life. And no one can take that away from you.

Look around you. Have you ever noticed how authors sort of seem to "strut their stuff?" Call it confidence! They tend to carry themselves a little bit differently because they, as well as others, perceive them as different. It's not ego, but the knowledge that they are viewed differently because they are the expert in their field.

Credibility and esteem are what give authors this little "strut." This is an invaluable tool, which used properly, can translate into $$$. When your customers trust their source, it makes it possible for them to make important decisions in their business.

The trust and authority granted to authors is already formed in the minds of the public, as well as the media. This knowledge is worth more than a king's ransom! This knowledge should be the foremost reason for becoming an author. Like I stated earlier, it's all about the new opportunities, the previously closed doors opening, and enhanced business relationships that being an author creates. All this answers the question of "Why should I become a published author?"

Think about it. Would you rather work with an "Average Joe," or an "Author/Expert?" Of course you'd rather do business with the expert! So would the majority of the population. Writing a book will allow you to STAND OUT from your competition....and put you at the level of all the other leaders that you have admired.

The Pen Is Mightier

Now I could sit here and give you a thousand reasons how being a written author will open doors for you, or how easy it is to make you an author, or to give you the benefits of being an author, but I'd like to tell a story that's even more powerful than all the benefits I could give you.

A while back a friend of ours was offered a chance at a job building websites for a major electrical firm. Dave wasn't sure about going for the interview, because he was already putting in long hours at his business. But this was an awesome opportunity for rebuilding and monitoring the entire website for a major firm and all their branches.

One day I was talking with Dave about the power of being a published author and what it would do not only for his business, but also for his credibility. After much cajoling, I finally convinced him to let us do a book for him.

He never realized how much that book would eventually impact his life.

Dave was the third of three candidates interviewed, but by a little "dumb luck" he was aware of the proposals from the other two candidates. Not really wanting the job because he had so little free time, he raised his proposal several thousand dollars. Going into the interview feeling confident that he would *not* get the job, Dave went in very relaxed, introduced himself, and proceeded to hand out his book as his business card. Even though the interview went well, Dave figured that with his proposal being the highest, surely it would be going into the "rejection" file.

Two days later he received a call letting him know that indeed, the job was his. He was speechless and confused. Why did they hire the most expensive person? He knew he was good and could do the job, but did he have the time? After weighing the pros and cons, he figured he could use the extra money, and the job was not very difficult for him, so he accepted the offer.

About a month later he was talking with the Senior VP and came right out and asked him why he was hired. The answer shocked him. The Senior VP said "We are a billion dollar company. Money is really no object to us, so money was not the issue when we decided to hire someone. You were the only one who came into the interview with their own book. This showed us that you had knowledge about your field, took pride in your work, and that you were the expert that we needed." He also went on to say that "the head of the division still had his book sitting on his credenza."

It took a while for this to sink in, but once it did, Dave called me and apologized for the hard time he gave me about doing the book, and explained the conversation he had with the Senior VP. He said "you were so right. Many times I took hours wooing potential clients, only to be rejected. Here I walked in with a book, and almost immediately they made up their mind that I was the right person for the job. Incredible!"

Dave's only struggle at that point was how he was going to work on this project, while keeping his other clients happy. Well, the increase in money from the new job allowed him to bring in some extra help, which freed him up for his new client. With the extra help, he was also able to take in a few more clients as well.

Dave is still doing work with the Company, hired more associates, gained more clients, actually works less hours, and makes more money.

Do you think that Dave would have gotten the job if he didn't have his book? Maybe, maybe not. But he now credits the fact that his credibility actually came from being a published author.

The bottom line is this: *being a published author automatically makes you an expert.* If you want an advantage over your competitors....then become a published author and brand yourself as the business expert in your niche.

There is no greater branding, or client enticement, than being a published author.

Become a published author today.

Payday To Playday

About Carolyn Lewis, *The Book Diva*

Carolyn Lewis knew many years ago the power of the written word. From writing articles for her local newspaper, to becoming Sr. Editor, to doing interviews for a local radio station, she got an early start into the publishing world. But as we all know, sometimes it takes the long way to get to where we need to be.

For many years Carolyn was side-tracked in the corporate world. But through hard work and dedication, she made her way up the corporate ladder at each company she graced. From her first brush with the internet, to her management skills of launching AOL discs to your mail box, she has a diverse business background in such areas as finance, marketing, management, human resources and production, including owning and operating her own businesses.

In 2002, Carolyn joined her husband Mike in his Land Development Company, overseeing their $100 million business as Chief Financial Officer. Unfortunately, the real estate down-turn culminated in their $60 million bankruptcy. Now it was time to re-invent not only their businesses, but their lives.

Payday To Playday

After a diligent review of various business opportunities, the potential to impact people's lives with a published book was by far the most exciting choice. Coupled with the enjoyment she receives from working with other professionals, her publishing background, as well as the obvious choice that this was a great business model, convinced her that this is where she wants to be.

With a true passion and desire for helping entrepreneurs to "take it to the next level," Carolyn is here to assist you in producing your printed book, therefore accomplishing your goal to become the expert in your field.

Contact Carolyn directly at **clewis@nomadceo.com** for more information on how you, too, can join the ranks as a published author, or visit **www.nomadceo.com.**

"*Money coming in says I've made the right marketing decisions.*"

~Adam Osborne~

Your Chance To Work
With David Cavanagh

If You Are A Promoter, Speaker,
Marketer Or Entrepreneur,
Then We Need To Work

Together In 2014

WE NEED TO TALK NOW

What kind of things would you dream to change, if you were given the chance to surround yourself with the **best internet marketers, speakers, promoters** and **joint venture partners**?

And I'm not just referring to the best experts in your suburb, state or country - no way - I'm offering you the chance to be in an online community with the **best Internet Marketing group in the World!**

Go to:

www.AfterTheCruise.com

And click "Join" for your FREE Membership that'll commence in February 2014

Work online and offline with
David Cavanagh
at World Wide events, seminars and
workshops